FRC
STRESSED

TO ZEN

A Mindfulness Journey for College Success and Beyond

JILL M. SOMMERS

Dream UP! Media
© 2024 by Jill M. Sommers

Published in Boulder, Colorado

Manuscript prepared by Melissa Killian of Killian Creative
Book design by Rob Williams of InsideOut Creative Arts, Inc.

ISBN: 979-8-9914502-0-1

Printed in the United States of America

To every "Tyler"
who hears the calling for a life fueled
by authenticity, intention,
and mindfulness . . .

And to Charlie,
for your unwavering belief
and endless love.

Contents

Your Mindfulness Journey:
Is this the most beneficial practice
for you at this time?

A mindfulness journey will bring you closer to your physical sensations, thoughts, and feelings. This self-awareness journey might feel uncomfortable at times, which is normal. However, if you find you are dealing with conflicting thoughts and emotions due to circumstances unique to you, this might not be the right time to dive deep into a mindfulness practice. If you are experiencing psychiatric challenges such as psychosis, depression, anxiety, trauma, post-traumatic stress disorder (PTSD), or bipolar disorder, this might be a challenging period to embark upon a journey into the practices of mindfulness. While substantial evidence suggests that mindfulness can be beneficial for these health challenges, it is advisable to consult with your mental health provider to determine if now is an appropriate time for you to engage in an exploration of mindfulness. If you choose to embark upon this journey, I encourage you to be especially aware of how the mindfulness practices feel for you. If they prove beneficial, continue to embrace them. If not, feel free to let them go. Remember, there are many paths to health and happiness.

INTRODUCTION

Life is fleeting. Don't waste a single moment of your precious life.
Wake up now! And now! And now!

—RUTH OZEKI

I had no idea what mindfulness was when I signed up for the Mind Body Awareness course," confided Tyler. "I thought we might light a candle, sit on the floor with our legs crossed, and maybe chant. I laughed at the idea of taking a class like this, but since I could get two credits for it, I decided to give it a go. In the end, I can honestly say it was the best course I took throughout my entire university experience. Building a mindfulness practice literally saved my life."

Perhaps, like Tyler, you've arrived at this book with a mix of curiosity and uncertainty, unsure of how you found yourself here or what exactly you're getting into. If you're holding this book, you're likely a young adult, possibly a college or university student. However, the wisdom and exercises within these pages transcend beyond college age. Regardless of your stage in life, you will benefit from the mindfulness practices and insights shared here.

I created this book with young adults in mind because this incredible stage of life is a whirlwind of potential, brimming with opportunities for personal growth and self-discovery. Even if you are not just starting out, you always have the power to cultivate positive habits that are the bedrock of lasting fulfillment and well-being.

If you are a young adult, you stand at the crossroads of numerous transitions, whether you're just now diving into your college experience, navigating its turbulent middle, or preparing to step into the world beyond academia into the dawn of a new career. This is a time when you're not only studying subjects, but also crafting the narrative of who you are and who you aspire to become. You're making pivotal decisions about academics, self-care, social connections, and community involvement.

It's precisely during this transformative period that embracing mindfulness can be a game-changer. By integrating mindfulness into your daily life, you'll equip yourself with invaluable tools to navigate challenges, foster resilience, and cultivate a balanced and thriving existence. You're not just preparing for a successful life; you're building habits for a meaningful and joyous life for decades to come.

I am neither a scientist nor sage. I don't conduct lab research on brains or clinically study people's behavior. My "lab" has been in the classroom with college students, coaching teenage and adult athletes in sports, and professionally coaching clients of all types seeking to expand their lives. For forty years, I've had the incredible opportunity to work alongside more than 7,000 individuals eager to explore and broaden their understanding of life. Along the way, I've deepened my knowledge through various graduate programs, certifications, and invaluable lessons from life itself. Sharing concepts and tools with my students and clients has been an absolute privilege. It is powerful and enlightening to witness the lasting changes that occur when individuals embrace a mindful approach.

This journey has revealed certain undeniable truths. One such truth is that the "old school" mentality of endlessly working harder and longer as the sole path to success is failing us. The "busy is better," work-harder approach fosters a disconnection from our needs and desires, leading to burnout, stress, illness, mental health challenges, and *decreased* productivity.

Our world has accelerated dramatically over the past thirty years, driven by modern technology and the rise of the internet. While these advancements have brought many benefits, they have also pulled us away from our centers, distancing us from healthful thoughts, emotions, actions, nutrition, and genuine connection. It's time to rethink our approach and prioritize a lifestyle that fosters balance, well-being, and mindfulness.

Mindfulness offers an alternative—a way to cultivate awareness, focus, and inner peace. It allows us to work smarter, live more fully, achieve our goals with joy and ease, *and* connect with self and others in heartfelt and meaningful ways.

It is time to cultivate a Mindfulness Movement, and your journey from stressed to Zen is the pivotal first step toward living a more balanced, peaceful, and fulfilling life. This transformation will not only enhance your own well-being, but will also create a ripple effect that positively impacts everyone around you.

I am thrilled to share the principles and practices that I live by and have taught my students and clients over the years. If you commit to openly engaging with these practices, you will notice a transformative shift within yourself. You'll learn how to break free from obstructive thought patterns, navigate difficult emotions, and make more conscious choices. This process of self-discovery will bring greater joy, boost your confidence, and instill a deep belief in your capabilities that should last a lifetime. Abbie, a former student once shared,

> *Life is busy and full of distractions. It is easy to get caught up and pulled away from who I am. Learning different ways to reset and ease my mind, I was able to fully grasp what was most important to me rather than getting confused by what everyone else thought was important. Recognizing that "what I want" and "what others want" are often completely opposite, I learned how to give myself permission to follow my desires. This awareness and action eased my stress tremendously and had such a positive impact on me that it will be a guiding force for me my entire life.*

The journey of mindfulness is something that anyone can embark upon, regardless of where they currently are in life. Using simple tools to live with more awareness, intention, and balance won't stop the fluctuations that life brings, but it will empower you to navigate through its ups, downs, and dull status quo like a superhero. And the best part is, you don't have to be an expert or have any specific background to start.

By actively engaging in this mindfulness journey, you are investing in *you,* and equipping yourself with invaluable resources that will positively impact your college experience *and beyond*. This journey will provide you with a wide range of tools and techniques to empower you to discover what works best for you, not only for your mindfulness practice, but also for your life. As you navigate through the chapters, I encourage you to fully engage in the exercises, even if you initially feel some resistance. Many students have shared that they were surprised by the positive impact of the practices, despite their initial hesitation.

From Stressed to Zen is a journey that leads you through three major segments. In Part One, you will learn about the foundations of mindfulness, including the power of breath, establishing a beginner's mind, learning how to be present, and deepening your connection to your "whole" self.

After establishing these important foundations, Part Two helps you strengthen your journey with powerful practices—from setting clear intentions to embracing gratitude, connecting with nature, utilizing visualization, to dropping into meditation.

In Part Three, you are encouraged to deepen your practice by engaging in a series of mindfulness challenges designed to help you integrate everything you have learned and practiced.

Throughout my years of learning and teaching, one thing has become evident to me: words alone don't teach—experience does. Therefore, each chapter in this book offers not only written content, but also opportunities to immerse yourself in the practices and principles discussed. The "Let's Practice" section guides you through experiential exercises that directly correlate with the chapter's content, inviting you to apply what you've read. Additionally, each chapter's "Journal Prompts" provide opportunities for self-reflection, helping you internalize and personalize your journey.

Throughout, you'll find real-life examples from the stories of those I've had the honor of working with (their names have been changed to protect their identity). To every one of them, I hold deep gratitude and feel truly humbled to have been a witness and guide along their unique paths.

My heartfelt wish for you is to wholeheartedly fall in love with every aspect of this book—from its look and feel, to the inspiring content, engaging stories, and insightful guidance it holds. I hope it becomes so near and dear to your heart that it effortlessly becomes your go-to source for comfort during challenging times, guidance when you need direction, and self-reflection to deepen your understanding of who you are.

My recommendation is to journey through the book from start to finish, beginning with the foundations and gradually moving forward, allowing yourself time to absorb, practice, and reflect. However, sometimes you might feel drawn to a specific chapter because that content resonates with you today. If that's the case, follow your instinct and dive into that chapter.

From Stressed to Zen will help you develop a mindfulness practice that will not only serve you through your college years, but also beyond into the next chapters of your life. Ultimately, I intend to support you on your path toward overall life mastery. By immersing yourself in the wisdom and practices contained in this book, you have the opportunity to cultivate a profound sense of self-awareness, find inner peace, and thrive in all areas of your life; use it as both your companion and compass to navigate life with grace and clarity.

Let's walk this path together, each step a mindful one, creating a ripple effect of peace and presence that can change the world and create a Mindfulness Movement. By incorporating this invitation into your life, you can spark not only individual change, but a collective transformation toward a more mindful and compassionate self and society.

So, my friend, I invite you to open yourself up to the possibility of a transformative journey. Let this book be your trusted companion, and may it bring you comfort, guidance, self-reflection, and ultimately, help you master the art of living with greater self-awareness and well-being—all so you can . . .

Love deeper
Fly higher
See clearer
Burn brighter
Feel more than [you] ever did before.

—MICHAEL FRANTI

From Stressed to Zen
Mindfulness Pre-Assessment

Before we embark on this transformative journey together, let's take a moment for some self-reflection. This mindfulness pre-assessment is designed to help you gain a clearer picture of where you stand right now. Think of it as a personal check-in to understand your current state of mindfulness. By reflecting on your answers, you'll not only gain insight into your present habits, but also create a benchmark to measure your progress as we move through this journey.

Let's get started on your path from stressed to Zen!

> **Instructions:** For each statement below, please circle the number that best describes how often you experience each situation.

1 = Rarely or Never | **2** = Occasionally | **3** = Sometimes
4 = Often | **5** = Almost Always

1. AWARENESS OF BREATH: I consciously notice and focus on my breath throughout the day.

1   2   3   4   5

2. ENGAGING WITH NATURE: I spend time in nature to relax and rejuvenate.

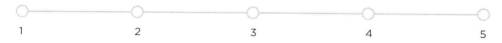

1   2   3   4   5

3. NONJUDGMENTAL OBSERVATION: I observe my thoughts and feelings without judging them.

1   2   3   4   5

4. EATING FOR HEALTH AND ENERGY: I make mindful food choices that support my overall health and energy levels.

1 — 2 — 3 — 4 — 5

5. PRESENT MOMENT AWARENESS: I fully experience and engage with the present moment, rather than getting lost in thoughts about the past or future.

1 — 2 — 3 — 4 — 5

6. STRESS RESPONSE: When I feel stressed, I use mindfulness techniques to help calm myself down.

1 — 2 — 3 — 4 — 5

7. NURTURING SLEEP: I prioritize getting enough restful sleep and maintaining a consistent sleep routine.

1 — 2 — 3 — 4 — 5

8. ACCEPTANCE: I accept things as they are without immediately trying to change them.

1 — 2 — 3 — 4 — 5

9. EMOTIONAL AWARENESS: I am aware of my emotions as they arise and can name them accurately.

1 — 2 — 3 — 4 — 5

10. ASKING FOR HELP: I reach out for support when I need help or am feeling overwhelmed.

1 — 2 — 3 — 4 — 5

11. BODY AWARENESS: I pay attention to physical sensations in my body without judging them.

1 2 3 4 5

12. MINDFUL COMMUNICATION: I listen fully when others are speaking, without planning my response while they talk.

1 2 3 4 5

13. REACTIVITY: I notice when I'm reacting automatically and try to respond more mindfully.

1 2 3 4 5

14. COMPASSION: I treat myself with kindness and understanding when I'm going through a difficult time.

1 2 3 4 5

Scoring Instructions: To reveal your overall mindfulness profile, simply add up the numbers you've circled for each statement. This total will give you a sense of where you currently stand on the path toward greater mindfulness. Think of it as a snapshot that captures your present state, providing a foundation for growth and reflection as we dive deeper into the course.

- **14-28:** You might be new to mindfulness or find it challenging to incorporate into your daily life. This course will offer you valuable tools and practices to develop your mindfulness skills.

- **29-42:** You have some mindfulness awareness, but there's room for growth. This course will help you deepen your practice and develop more mindful habits.

- **43-56:** You're fairly aware and practicing mindfulness regularly. This course will help you refine your techniques and broaden your understanding.

- **57-70:** You have a strong mindfulness practice already! This course will offer advanced insights and practices to enhance your journey.

Thank you for taking the time to complete this pre-assessment. Keep it handy—you'll find it helpful to refer to as you progress. Mindfulness is a continuous journey, not a fixed destination. Wherever you're starting from today, embrace this as an opportunity for growth and expansion. Each step you take is a valuable part of your own personal Mindfulness Movement.

PART 1

BUILDING
FOUNDATIONS

ONE

THE MAGIC OF
MINDFULNESS

*Mindfulness is awareness that arises through paying attention,
on purpose, in the present moment, non-judgmentally.*

—JON KABAT-ZINN

The anticipation had been building for weeks as I prepared for the first day of classes at the University of Wisconsin, Milwaukee (UWM). At that time, I had been creating and teaching mindfulness courses for more than a decade to students at all stages of their academic journey, from first-year freshmen to graduating seniors. As a new semester begins, my excitement is palpable, brimming with anticipation for the transformative experiences that lie ahead.

As the students trickled into the classroom, I greeted each one with warmth and a genuine smile. I had carefully designed an icebreaker exercise that would foster trust and create a sense of camaraderie among the students.

Once everyone had arrived, I closed the doors to create an intimate and safe environment. We began with introductions, followed by the icebreaker exercise, which filled the room with laughter and the feeling of connection. Next, I guided them through a relaxation exercise, allowing them to unwind and settle into the present moment.

With only a few minutes left in the class, I noticed a student standing outside the glass door, seeking entry. I invited him into the room for the remainder of the class. He introduced himself, and while he seemed apprehensive at first, he quickly showed a genuine desire to engage and immerse himself in the Mind Body Awareness course.

From that day on, Tyler's dedication was evident. He arrived early to class and stayed late, helping me rearrange the room before and after class. He shared that he had a learning disability, and because he often needed concepts repeated, he wasn't afraid to seek clarification. Not only was he a diligent student, but he also became a source of inspiration and encouragement for his classmates. Tyler had quickly won me over with his open mind and willingness to learn.

It wasn't until I received Tyler's final project that I truly understood the depth of his struggles. His project required self-reflection, encompassing his past thoughts, behaviors, and actions, as well as visualizing and clarifying his aspirations for a brighter future. It was in the closing statement of his project that I discovered the overwhelming impact our course had had on his life. With tears welling in my eyes, I read his words: "Thank you for all you taught me in this course. I learned so much about my thoughts and how they steer my beliefs and actions. So much, that I no longer feel like killing myself."

Tyler's story serves as a powerful testament to the transformative impact of mindfulness—in other words, having an open mind to learn, developing self-understanding, increasing awareness of thoughts and emotions, and intentionally choosing actions that place you in alignment with your values.

By incorporating mindfulness into his daily routine, Tyler became acutely aware of how his thoughts, many of them negative and limiting, shaped his beliefs about himself. He learned how to reframe and redirect these thoughts intentionally and purposefully. He discovered that his thoughts fueled his emotions and realized that by aligning his thoughts with his desires, he could transform his emotional state.

With this newfound understanding, Tyler recognized that he had the power to steer the direction of his life; he was able to make choices that aligned with his values and desired emotional state. Mindfulness became his compass, guiding him towards a more fulfilling and empowered life.

When you know better, you can do better.
—MAYA ANGELOU

You might also be navigating through various obstacles and pressures that feel overwhelming. Tyler's journey highlights the benefits of practicing mindfulness as a means to steer through these challenges from a place of power. By cultivating self-awareness and consciously choosing your thoughts and actions, you can harness the ability to shape your own journey and create a life that resonates with your authentic self.

While external circumstances may pose difficulties, your mindset and emotional resilience play a vital role in overcoming them. By developing a mindfulness practice, you can build the inner strength and emotional well-being that will help you navigate your college years *and beyond* with more intention, direction, and self-compassion. Ultimately, Tyler's story invites you to become the conscious author of your own life, steering your course toward a brighter and more fulfilling future. As you make your journey from stressed to Zen, watch how Tyler's story unfolds, offering valuable insights and mindfulness practices that redirect his path from chaos to ease.

A Beautiful Tapestry of Moments

In the journey of life, we encounter a beautiful tapestry of moments. Some moments are filled with joy and wonder, while others can be quite the opposite—stressful, upsetting, and draining. Sometimes they are mundane and monotonous, while other times they can be devastating or traumatic. It's the frustration of a never-ending commute to school, the occasional clash with a roommate, unexpected bills that throw you off balance, marathon study sessions that leave you depleted, nagging illnesses that drain your energy, the sting of criticism from professors, heart-wrenching breakups, and the constant juggling of school, work, and self-care. Ah yes, a "beautiful" tapestry of moments, for sure.

Whether it's the small yet consistent annoyances, or those hard-hitting challenges, your belief in your ability to navigate life's ups and downs will naturally waver. However, it is the belief in yourself and your ability to be the "author of your story"—the "navigator of your journey"—that will eventually become your superpower.

The art and skill of mindfulness, which requires consistent practice, will help you tap in to that power. Mindfulness may seem complex, but it is not complicated. It is the simple but diligent practice of being fully present and engaged in the current moment, without judgment or distraction. It involves paying close attention to your thoughts, feelings, bodily sensations, and the surrounding environment with a gentle, nurturing attitude. Rather than letting your mind wander or dwell on the past or future, mindfulness encourages focusing on what is happening right now.

The exciting part is that this mindfulness journey offers you the opportunity to cultivate your own inner treasures. Think of it as building your very own treasure box filled with valuable tools and goodies. In this treasure box, you will find qualities like empathy, self-understanding, and self-compassion. You will discover a sense of security, confidence, and resilience within yourself. Additionally, you will develop essential interpersonal skills, feel more comfortable in your own body, and find a sense of balance and ease in your life, leading to an inner state of Zen.

"What the heck is Zen?" you might be wondering. In general terms, Zen signifies a sense of calm, simplicity, and harmony. It is a state of being in alignment with one's true self—a state in which you cultivate a mindful presence and live fully in each moment. Being able to tap in to your inner Zen—especially when everything around you feels chaotic—is what creating a mindfulness practice is all about.

Simply put, mindfulness is the practice we use to arrive at Zen—a state of profound calm and harmony. Through mindfulness, we learn to tune in to the present moment, paying close attention to our thoughts, emotions, and surroundings with acceptance and without judgment. This practice helps us navigate life's inevitable chaos and distractions, leading us to a place of inner tranquility and balance. By consistently integrating mindfulness into our daily routines, we gradually create a pathway to our own inner Zen, enabling us to live more fully and peacefully.

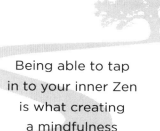

Being able to tap in to your inner Zen is what creating a mindfulness practice is all about.

You might be thinking, "Can I fit something else into my bursting-at-the-seams schedule?" Rest assured, now is the optimal time to integrate mindfulness into your routine. The beauty of this practice lies in its simplicity and adaptability. Adopting mindfulness will not monopolize your time; instead, it will seamlessly weave into your current lifestyle, enhancing your moments in school, with friends, in athletics, while studying, taking exams, while at work, or while interviewing for your post-college career. What's more, the impact of practicing mindfulness will remain with you long after you graduate from college.

When you incorporate a mindfulness practice into your daily life, you perceive the world (and yourself) more deeply. You gain a deeper grasp of your mental, emotional, and physical environments, and this increased awareness enables you to consciously *respond* to life's many challenges rather than unconsciously *react* to them. This is an invaluable life skill that will give you a powerful advantage in a reactive world.

Things are always happening—and are always going to happen. Accepting life "as it is," is fundamental to mindfulness; life is not a perfect path, and that is perfectly okay. Recognizing that life will always have highs and lows is not only a fleeting insight but also part of your personal development and evolution. This thoughtful approach inevitably produces a more profound sense of harmony and serenity that you'll find permeates every aspect of your existence.

Practicing mindfulness in your college years will help you create your own sense of peace and well-being—and will serve you well in all your future endeavors. As you continue along your academic path, consider mindfulness to be a trusty ally that will support you in building a composed and happy life.

Let's explore the many benefits of engaging in a mindfulness practice. Feel free to jot down any sparks of inspiration or ideas that catch your attention in the margins. Alternatively, you may wish to pause and reflect in your personal journal as you journey through these insights.

The Limitless Benefits of Mindfulness

There is no end to the benefits that scientific study is finding associated with mindfulness, which makes it an increasingly tempting discipline to adopt. Over the years, numerous studies have been conducted exploring the effectiveness of mindfulness practices. These studies have delved into various aspects of mindfulness, including its impact on mental health, stress reduction, emotional well-being, and overall quality of life. Research findings show that incorporating a mindfulness practice into our daily routine is not only beneficial to our mental and emotional health, but to our physical health as well. Yet centuries before any scientific studies existed, various cultures cultivated mindfulness as a regular practice in their traditions.

Countless centuries of practical application and anecdotal evidence have shaped an understanding of mindfulness as a powerful tool for personal growth, self-awareness, and inner transformation. The combination of historical wisdom and scientific inquiry provides a robust foundation for us to embrace mindfulness and explore its profound potential.

There's no denying the beneficial effects of mindfulness on mental health. Studies on the effects of mindfulness have shown significant improvements in relation to anxiety and depression. You can develop emotional control, stress resilience, lower cortisol levels—the iconic stress hormone—and decrease anxiety by engaging in regular mindfulness practices. Furthermore, people who frequently engage in mindfulness practices have been shown to improve cognitive function as well as improve focus and attention span.

Mindfulness can also positively influence physical health. Let's not forget that the benefits of mindfulness extend beyond the realms of mental and emotional well-being. The emerging scientific evidence indicates that mindfulness also impacts your physiological health. It has been associated with tangible improvements in lowering blood pressure, boosting immune function, aiding in pain management, and improving sports performance.

More importantly, mindfulness grounds you spiritually. It's important to acknowledge that the true power of mindfulness reaches beyond either the physical or mental/emotional realms, to something more transcendent. We're talking about ascending to a higher level of Zen! What do I mean by a higher level of Zen? It's when the practice of mindfulness connects you with your inner, intrinsic self, unraveling those deep existential questions—enabling you to explore richer dimensions of your spirituality and deeper personal growth. It is an opportunity to access a feeling of harmony, serenity, transcendence, and calm that goes beyond the confines of daily existence.

Let's take a look at ten primary "**Zen Benefits**" (or "Zen Bens," for short) that you will experience while integrating mindfulness into your daily life:

1. Self-Discovery. Alright, let's cut to the chase. When it comes to finding genuine happiness and inner peace, the secret sauce lies in getting to know your Self (with a capital *S*, because we're talking about the authentic Self here—the one that goes beyond the structured ego). Creating a distinctive mindfulness practice that reflects your uniqueness is your VIP pass to an amazing voyage of Self-discovery.

2. Deep & Lasting Fulfilment. Practicing mindfulness techniques helps calm the busy mind (monkey mind) and clears away cluttered thoughts, allowing you to connect with your authentic Self. Knowledge from your authentic Self empowers you to put your health first and gradually push aside the negative effects of fear, greed, manipulation, and coercion. By nurturing this inner connection, you embark on a transformative journey that goes beyond cultural pressures, leading to deeper and lasting fulfillment. This bond creates a solid foundation for making decisions: helping you to know what deserves your "yes" and what deserves your "no."

3. Authentic Happiness. Incorporating mindfulness practices into your daily routine empowers you to rise above the all-too-common pitfalls of "running with the herd," by intentionally choosing thoughts, feelings, actions, and behaviors that set you up for your happiest and most fulfilling life. Did you know that 86% of Americans say they live an unhappy life? Yep, you read that right! So, go the extra mile by intentionally choosing who you follow, who you ask advice from, and who you decide to model your life after. Choose instead to be part of that unique and uplifting 14% who truly live a happy life. Why settle for unhappiness merely to blend in with the discontented 86%?

Go the extra mile; it's never crowded there.

—WAYNE DYER

4. Genuine Joy. Have you ever experienced the transformation of something that used to feel mundane, but has now gained new significance and brings you genuine joy? Maybe it's the simple act of savoring a meal, the rhythm of your footsteps during a leisurely walk, or even something as basic as taking a breath. It's as if these seemingly ordinary activities have suddenly become profound sources of contentment, inviting you to appreciate the beauty of just being instead of constantly feeling the need to do something to find meaning in the moment. It's like finding a hidden treasure in the simplicity of everyday life. Mindfulness practices provide you with the foundation to make this a consistent part of your daily experience.

5. Boundless Energy. As you tune in to your authentic Self, you uncover a treasure trove of thoughts and emotions beyond the realm of negativity. Oh, I know how tempting it can be to get caught up in all the doom and gloom around you: news reports, social conversations, even the barrage of assignments you need to submit every week. But fear not! With a sprinkle of mindful awareness, you have the power to behold the wonders that lie beyond: joy, beauty, hopefulness, boundless energy, and meaningful connections. The practice of mindfulness helps you shift your focus so you can see all of it—from the challenging to the wonderful.

6. Empowered Focus. Saying goodbye to those sneaky distractions that continually find their way into your life becomes effortless because you have built a knowing of what you want, what you like, and how you want to feel. Like discovering an inner GPS, you are able to build your own navigational system based on your own true north. Too often we don't realize how little distractions play games with our mind. You know, the ones that make it so easy to avoid spending quality time on your studies, attending classes, connecting with friends, or being with family—and even tending to your amazing Self. It's almost as if they have a secret agenda to keep you from doing the things that would make you the happiest, the proudest, and the most alive.

Distractions often come with justifications such as, "I have to check Instagram to stay in the loop," or "I should call Olivia to show I care" (even if I secretly don't). Let's not forget, "I need to stay informed about the world's problems by watching the news," or "I have to go out with this group; I mean, what if I miss out on something epic?" But here's a mindful secret for you: When you become aware of these distractions and the fear that fuels them, you gain the power to chuck them out the window and live life authentically. No more hiding behind what others are doing or pretending to care about things you couldn't care less about. You're free to embrace self-awareness and experience the true empowerment of living life on your own terms, making space for genuine self-discovery. You are able to say "yes" to studying and "no" to that extra night out, because you are clear about what you truly want from life—or "yes" to hanging out with certain friends and "no" to hours of mindless scrolling, because you know what truly fills your cup.

7. Freedom to Change. When it comes to connecting with your Self, it is quite common to feel uneasy about it. It's as if there is a little voice in your head warning you that if you do this, there will be changes. Let's face it, with change comes change. (Stay with me here.) When you choose to change the way you're thinking, speaking and behaving, things cannot *not* change. But the truth is, those changes can be powerful. We're talking about releasing layers of anxiety, depression, neediness, feelings of unworthiness, limited intuition, impulsive behavior, a quick temper, fear, greed, anger, abandonment issues, those out-of-control reactions, unhealthy habits, and repetitive patterns that lead to undesirable outcomes, negative self-talk, and oh my, so much of that limiting belief system—aka BS. Letting go of all that baggage can open up a world of freedom and growth for you now and forever.

8. Contagious Enthusiasm. "Annie, Annie, are you okay?" Remember those CPR classes where you frantically shook the dummy named Annie, yelling "Annie, Annie, are you okay?" Practicing mindfulness can give you a similar burst of excitement that makes you want to shake the world awake. It's like experiencing a profound alignment that fills you with the urge to share the goodness. And the beauty is, when you share from this centered place of alignment, your message is one that uplifts and energizes others.

9. Endless Waves of Calm. When you release the need to constantly prove yourself, please others, and seek validation, a magical thing happens; you enter into—and ride—a big, beautiful wave of calm. In that state of calmness, you're able to fully embrace the present moment. You become one with your creativity and easily dive deep into introspection. It's like riding a blissful wave of peace. Mindfulness practices not only help you feel this bliss while in the midst of a practice session, but that wave of calmness continues to fuel you throughout your day, helping you navigate the highs and the lows.

10. Profound Alignment. Mindfulness increases your level of awareness of everything—your Self, those around you, your environment—everything. Now that you are more aware of all that impacts you, negatively and positively, you are more discerning about where you choose to spend your time and energy. Gone are the days of feeling obligated to do things you "should" or hang out with people who leave you feeling zapped. You're unleashing your inner superhero and making choices that light you up. There's no more "should'ing" all over yourself because that's just messy. Instead, you're embracing the joy of living in alignment with what truly fuels your soul.

Mindset and Mood State

Before we wrap up our discussion about mindfulness, I would be remiss if I didn't touch on two crucial components—*mindset* and *mood state*. For our focus together, we define *mindset* as the attitudes, beliefs, and perceptions that shape how you think. It's the lens through which you see and interpret your experiences and everything happening around you. Your mindset has a huge influence on your approach to life, affecting how you handle stress, obstacles, and opportunities.

Now, get this—research shows you have roughly 60,000 thoughts per day, and a whopping 95% of them are the same old repeats from the day before. That means just 5% of your thoughts are new! This goes to show how much repetitive thinking dominates your mental space and highlights why mindfulness practices are so important. By being more mindful, you can become aware of these patterns and start changing before thoughts that don't serve you well.

And here's something even more interesting: Your beliefs are just thoughts you keep thinking over and over again. So, while beliefs might seem rock solid and real, it's important to remember they are the result of thinking the same thought, whether the thought is true or not.

Mood state is how you are feeling in the present moment (or during a sustained period). Your mood state can influence your perceptions, thoughts, and behaviors. What is valuable to understand here is there is a direct link between your mindset and your mood state. Thoughts literally shape your emotions and trigger chemical shifts in your body. Imagine you're thinking about a stressful deadline. Your brain perceives this thought as a threat, activating your fight-or-flight response. This causes the release of stress hormones like cortisol and adrenaline, leading to increased heart rate, shallow breathing, and tensed muscles.

On the flip side, think about a happy memory. Your brain responds by releasing feel-good chemicals like serotonin and dopamine, which create a sense of well-being and relaxation. This chemical cocktail not only changes how you feel, but also positively impacts your physical state—lowering your heart rate, easing tension, and even boosting your immune system.

The takeaway here is profound: Your thoughts are not just abstract notions—they are dynamic forces that create real physical changes in your body. Becoming mindful of your thoughts gives you the power to influence your emotions and the chemical shifts in your body, steering your life toward greater balance and joy.

Now, the question is, "Who is in control of your thoughts?" Is it some magical puppeteer pulling your strings? Is it your parents, your roommates, your significant other, your professor, or your boss? Absolutely not! It is *you*! *You* are in control of your thoughts, and therefore *you* are in control of your emotions.

This understanding is crucial because it puts you back in the driver's seat of your life. The practice of mindfulness will help you create awareness of your thoughts and build the ability to shift, redirect, and steer them—and consequently your emotions—in ways that serve you better.

Let's Practice . . .

Let's take a few moments to slow things down and practice noticing your thoughts. This practice helps you become aware of your thought patterns and the recurring themes in your thinking. By viewing your thoughts on paper, you can start recognizing which are helpful and which may be limiting.

1. **Set a timer for five minutes.** Write down all the thoughts that come to mind without filtering or judging them. Some of them might be to-do items, some might be judgments, while others might be memories. There is no right or wrong here.
2. **After five minutes, review your list.** Notice which thoughts are positive (P), which are neutral (N), and which are negative (NG). Place a *P* next to the positive, an *N* next to the neutral, and an *NG* next to the negative thoughts. Notice how each thought makes you feel as you are moving through the exercise.

Journal Prompts . . .

1. Something I realized about myself from taking the Mindfulness Assessment is . . .
2. The "Zen Bens" that spoke to me the loudest are . . . because . . .
3. From following my thoughts for five minutes, one aspect of my life that I want to enhance through mindfulness is . . .

Bringing It All Together

It is powerful to recognize the profound impact that observing your thoughts and emotions can have on your life. By regularly practicing mindfulness, you cultivate a heightened awareness that allows you to navigate life's challenges with a sense of calm and clarity. You can then redirect your thoughts and emotions so they serve you, rather than hinder you. This practice not only helps you manage stress and improve mental well-being, but also brings forth the timeless benefits of Zen, including genuine joy, contagious enthusiasm, and endless waves of calm. It puts you back in the driver's seat of your life, opening doors to heartfelt connections with Self and others. As you expand your mindfulness practice, you might just find you are no longer willing to settle for whatever comes your way. You are now the curator of your own life, handpicking experiences that resonate with the fabulous human being that you are. *You are living with Zen.*

Now that you have a grip on what mindfulness and Zen are all about, let's dive into the heartbeat of it all—your breath. Imagine having a powerful tool that's always with you, ready to bring instant calm and focus. That's exactly what mindful breathing can do. It's your gateway to staying grounded and present, no matter what life throws your way. When you're ready to explore this amazing practice, turn the page and let's get started!

TWO

THE FOUNDATION OF LIFE
YOUR BREATH

What has to be taught first is the breath.

—CONFUCIUS

Welcome to the foundational chapter of your mind-fulness journey: Your Breath. Before we dive in, let's take a mindful moment together. Pause and pay attention to your breath—breathe in, breathe out. Notice how your body responds. Maybe your belly expands, or your chest rises and falls. Feel the air as it comes in through your nostrils.

Isn't it remarkable how automatic breathing is? You don't have to consciously think about it, yet it keeps you alive, seamlessly regulated by your subconscious mind. This allows you to focus on other aspects of your life, like deciding what to eat next, prioritizing your homework, or planning your commute.

From nourishing your body to quieting your restless mind, from releasing emotional stress to connecting with your innermost self, breath is your anchor. It is the common thread that unites your human existence with the world around you. It is the glue that holds together all aspects of who you are. Consider this: Without breath, the brain can suffer irreversible damage within minutes. Each breath you take is critically important. Your breath is the simplest, yet most powerful tool you have.

This is a great time to pause and pay attention to your breath—take a moment to breathe in . . .and breathe out.

In this chapter, we will investigate the breath's power as a means of achieving greater awareness, resiliency, and harmony both within oneself and in the environment. We will begin by exploring the impact of your breath on your physical health to get a better understanding of what's happening, or not happening, on the physiological level.

Physiological Impacts of Your Breath

Breathing is the mechanism that enables both circulation and respiration, which work together as a dynamic pair. Oxygen enters your bloodstream as you breathe and travels throughout your entire body. You see, for your organs to perform at their peak, especially your brain, they require blood that is high in oxygen. But breathing does more for your body than transport oxygen; it helps your body get rid of carbon dioxide, a waste product that is produced by your cells. Imagine it as an exchange program taking place within your lungs. Your organs wouldn't be able to function if there wasn't this vital exchange of oxygen and carbon dioxide, and the circulation that comes with it. Either insufficient oxygen delivery, or inadequate removal of carbon dioxide, would severely impair the functioning of your organs.

Let's look at a few examples of complications that can arise in specific organs when your breathing is shortened or impaired:

Your Brain. Insufficient oxygen supply to the brain caused by poor breathing habits, such as slouching or bending over while studying, can lead to difficulties concentrating, memory issues, dizziness, and potential loss of consciousness. Consider that bothersome headache or persistent brain fog; might these be caused by your brain not getting the oxygen it needs? So before you reach for the aspirin or grab another cup of coffee, consider taking a moment to close your eyes and take a few deep, nourishing breaths. Although a small gesture, the effect can be significant.

The next time your mind feels sluggish, foggy, or absent, give it an oxygen boost. Your breath is a constant support system, one that is always with you, no matter where you go or what you're doing. It has no negative side effects and is completely free! In the Let's Practice section toward the end of this chapter, you'll have an opportunity to learn and practice a full-body breathing technique called "5-Phase Breathing." In the meantime, pause and pay attention to your breath—breathe in, breathe out.

Your Heart. For optimal operation, the muscles in your heart need a steady flow of oxygen. Reduced cardiac output, angina, irregular heartbeats, and heart muscle injury (myocardial infarction) can all result from low oxygen levels. Eventually, these conditions can cause heart failure (yikes, let's avoid this).

Charlie, a college junior, who was busy multi-tasking with a heavy school load, part-time job, and a busy social life was having "weird" chest pains. He ignored them for a couple of months, writing them off as not sleeping well or eating spicy food, until one day when they became so intense he decided to go to the campus clinic to check it out. After a complete check-up, the practitioner informed him that, physically, everything was fine, but the stress he was trying to manage was causing him to hold his breath and decrease the amount of oxygen he was sending to his heart. The prescription? Breathe deeply and often. This episode scared Charlie so much, he followed the doctor's orders and focused on taking deep breaths throughout the day, while rearranging his schedule to prioritize his mental and physical health. His "weird" chest pains subsided without any other interventions or medications. He was both surprised and relieved the remedy was so simple and within his control, reminding him that breath is a powerful force.

Your Respiratory System. Insufficient exhalation of carbon dioxide can affect lung function. The proper exchange of gasses can be impeded by severe asthma and chronic obstructive pulmonary disease (COPD), which can lead to breathing difficulties, a reduced capacity to withstand physical effort, and poor respiratory health. Are you aware that 11.7 million adult Americans suffer from COPD, and that many more suffer from the disease without realizing it? Yet it has been proven that often, these symptoms are caused by insufficient breathing.

Consider college student, Neil, as an example. After utilizing the 5-phase breathing technique for four weeks, Neil saw a significant improvement in his respiratory health. He only needed to use his inhaler once daily, down from an astounding four times per day. Full of enthusiasm, Neil exclaimed, "I'm so excited to see how much less I'll rely on my inhaler by week eight!" It's truly remarkable what intentional breathing can achieve!

Your Digestion. For the digestive system to work at its best, it needs a constant flow of oxygen. Insufficient oxygen levels can lead to several problems. One of those problems is the decreased absorption of nutrients. In the digestive system, oxygen is essential for the digestion and absorption of nutrients. Insufficient oxygen can inhibit the body's ability to absorb vital nutrients from food by impeding the digestive process.

In Western society, where there is a heavy emphasis on having a "flat stomach," it is very common for people to hold in their stomachs, whether deliberately or unintentionally. This abdominal tightness restricts the diaphragm's ability to expand and contract and prevents the lungs from being fully utilized, which ultimately prevents the best possible oxygen intake during breathing. This restricted breathing exacerbates conditions such as bloating, indigestion, slow bowel movements, and constipation by adding to the reduced oxygen flow to the digestive system. The muscle contractions that move waste products through the intestines can become feeble and ineffective when the digestive system is oxygen-starved. Severe constipation may arise as a result of irregular bowel movements and a buildup of stool in the colon.

Understanding the significance of taking full breaths can be a gamechanger. Allowing your abdomen to stretch and relax will significantly improve the efficacy of your breathing. This not only boosts your oxygen levels, but also supports a healthy digestive system.

Your Posture and Muscular Support. Using the right breathing techniques helps to improve your posture and activate your core muscles. The diaphragm, which is the main breathing muscle, can be used to stabilize the spine, maintain good posture, and lessen strain or imbalance in the muscles. The symptoms of low oxygen delivery to the muscles include weariness, weakened muscles, and a reduced capacity for physical activity. Additionally, soreness, cramping, and decreased muscle function can result from the buildup of carbon dioxide in the muscles when it is not properly removed.

Jan, a college freshman, didn't give much thought to the way they sat while studying. It wasn't until they participated in my Mind Body Awareness course that they became aware of how much they slouched while in class and while studying outside of class. They complained often of not being able to focus on school and homework, often felt sleepy, unfocused, and unable to pay attention. After bringing awareness to their posture, Jan decided to prioritize a more upright position while in class and while studying. "I cannot believe the difference this has made in my ability to focus and to stay more energized throughout my day," Jan declared. "It was difficult for me at first because I had to strengthen my core muscles, but as I focused attention on my position, my breath got fuller and my posture got taller. It was as if they were fueling one another. As my breath got bigger, my posture got bigger, which allowed me to breathe bigger."

Your Energy and Vitality. Your energy and vitality are crucial components that drive your progress and success in life. When you consciously increase the amount of oxygen you're able to intake through intentional deep breathing, you experience a surge in energy that makes it easier for you to fully engage in the moment, in the day, and in your life. With this renewed vitality, you're more likely to seek out new experiences, embark on adventures, and fully appreciate the richness life has to offer. This burst of energy opens doors to a world of possibilities, inviting you to enhance each moment with curiosity and excitement—better enabling you to overcome any obstacle along your path.

The next time you get a hint of fatigue or feel depleted, stop and pay attention to your breathing. Sit up tall, take that deep breath, and allow the rush of oxygen to rejuvenate your body. Why not do it now? Breathe in, breathe out.

Your Nervous System. Now that you understand how breathing impacts the levels of oxygen and carbon dioxide in your physical body, affecting particular organs and your overall energy levels, let's explore how breathing controls your neural system. It's amazing how something as basic as inhaling deeply can have a significant influence on your general state of mental health. For example, inducing slow, deep breathing promotes serenity and relaxation by activating the parasympathetic nervous system and applying the brakes to the stress response. Your blood pressure drops, your muscles relax, and your heart rate slows as you become more at peace—as if treating yourself to a brief getaway from the chaos of everyday pressures. On the other hand, when you take rapid, shallow breaths (also known as chest breathing), you stimulate the sympathetic nervous system, which is responsible for your fight-or-flight response. This can trigger heightened anxiety, racing thoughts, an increased heart rate, and an increase in muscle tension.

The balance between the sympathetic nervous system, which speeds things up, and the parasympathetic nervous system, which calms things down, is directly impacted by the way you breathe. Through deliberate breath control, you can access your regulating system's soothing abilities, which can assist you in finding peace despite the stresses of daily life. It's a power tool you can use to help you handle the ups and downs with more poise and resilience.

*You can't stop the waves but you can
learn to surf.*

—JON KABAT-ZINN

Through specific breathing techniques, you can further regulate your nervous system response. These practices not only bring you into the present moment (the only place where you have power), but they also enhance your mind-body connection, promoting a greater sense of self-awareness and emotional stability.

The great news here is that you have control over your "automatic" breath, which has a powerful influence on many biological and emotional factors. Yes, it is both automatic and manual. Think of it like the gears on a bicycle. Most of the time, when you're cruising along on flat terrain, you can let the bike do its thing, effortlessly pedaling without much thought. This is like your breath on automatic—steady, reliable, and keeping you going without needing your attention. But when you hit a hill or need to accelerate, you shift gears to adapt to the new challenge—like shifting your breath to manual mode. You consciously control it, making each inhale and exhale purposeful to power you through the up-hill struggle or to gain speed.

By learning to "shift gears" with your breath, you gain the ability to navigate the various terrains of life with more ease and control. Whether you're managing stress, needing a moment of calm, or even boosting your focus, mastering this shift can keep you balanced and resilient.

Meet Melinda, a self-proclaimed anxious college sopho-more studying architecture, who battled panic attacks and had not yet learned how to shift her proverbial breathing gears. She found herself caught in a relentless cycle of fear—starting with fearing the occurrence of more panic attacks—which, in turn, fueled her anxiety and intensified her fear of inducing another panic attack. However, during our med-itation course, Melinda embarked on a fascinating explora-tion of her breath. What she discovered was truly eye-opening: Instead of the issue stemming from not breathing deeply enough, as she first thought, Melinda discovered a deeper problem. She noticed she had trouble letting go of her breath, which made it difficult for her to inhale deeply. The exhale was the missing piece of the puzzle for her.

Continuing to practice her breathing and becoming more aware of her breath cycle, she discovered a long-stand-ing apprehension of letting go. This dread resulted from an unconscious fear of losing control, which finally caused her to inadvertently hold her breath. Her incapacity to suffi-ciently exhale and remove carbon dioxide created a red flag in her body, which ignited "worry hormones," leading to full-blown panic attacks.

Melinda's epiphany was the turning point that made clear the close relationship between her breathing, her anxi-ety, and her panic episodes. Equipped with this fresh insight, she now understands that the secret to taking back control of her breath, and eventually her nervous thoughts, is to prac-tice a deliberate and balanced exhale. This serves to highlight the importance of paying attention to both the inhale and the exhale. Maintaining equilibrium between the two promotes a healthy exchange of oxygen and carbon dioxide, which is good for your body and helps you feel emotionally stable. It is a function of equal opportunity. Inhale deeply. Exhale fully.

The next time you're feeling overwhelmed or seeking a moment of peace, remember that your breath is right there, ready to be your ally. Take a few intentional, deep, full breaths, allowing your nervous system to regulate, find balance, and pave the way to a calm, centered, and aligned version of yourself.

Take a moment now to pause and pay attention to your breath—breathe in, breathe out.

Intentional breathing opens your awareness to the life energy that moves through you and unites you with all living things.

Coming Into Alignment Spiritually

Breathing intentionally is a potent trigger for improving personal alignment and strengthening spiritual connection. You can develop a more transcendent awareness and presence by purposefully directing your breath, creating what feels like a sacred space within your consciousness. This deliberate breathing practice not only relieves tension and calms the mind, but it also opens the door to inner wisdom and intuition.

Breath is the key that unlocks the vast potential of our spiritual existence. It is through the intentional and mindful breath that we access inner peace, transcendental states, and profound connection to the universal energy.

—MICHAEL SINGER

As you engage in intentional breathing practices, you invite a state of calmness and tranquility, creating fertile ground for self-reflection and introspection. This sacred pause allows you to tune into your higher self, to tap in to your inner guidance, and to align with your deepest values and intentions.

Intentional breathwork can also help you develop a strong sense of oneness and connection with the environment. Intentional breathing opens your awareness to the life energy that moves through you and unites you with all living things. A profound sense of reverence and appreciation for the beauty and sacredness of existence is fostered by this relationship. By intentionally adding breathwork into your everyday practices, you create a deeper and more personal connection with a higher spiritual energy that permeates all life. These connections foster within you a stronger sense of purpose, inner serenity, and a more genuine expression of your soul and higher Self. Intentional breathing is the key to spiritual development, metamorphosis, and a more profound comprehension of your role in the grand scheme of things. By aligning your breath with your deepest goals and dreams, you open the door for inspiration and guidance to enter your life.

Remember to breathe.
It is, after all, the secret of life.

Taking a deep breath is natural and instinctual, yet along the journey of life, many of us lose the ability to fully engage with the power of our breath. The good news is, with just a little practice, the body will remember and easily return to the origin of the deep breath. Here are two easy-to-implement, powerful breath practices you can begin using right now.

Let's Practice . . .

The 5-Phase Breath

The 5-Phase Breath is our number one practice for bringing the Self back to center. It is simple to implement, can be done anywhere without anyone noticing, and is extremely effective at calming the nervous system. This breath, also called the yogic breath, is a full-body inhale and exhale. The five phases include inhaling through your nose, filling your belly, your lower chest, your upper chest, opening your throat, and then exhaling through an open mouth. Let's give it a try:

Begin with mindful preparation. Find a comfortable place to sit or lie down on your back. Let this place be warm, comfortable, safe, and free of distractions. Go ahead and get comfortable now. Place one hand on your stomach and the other hand on your chest. Notice the rise and fall of your natural breath. Bring your attention to this moment, allowing your breath to transport you inward. Notice everything you can about the inhale, exhale, and the space between the two.

1. Take in a deep inhale through your nose, allowing your belly to expand like a balloon filling with air.
2. On your next inhale, allow your belly to expand and then bring in a little more breath so your lower chest rises.
3. On your subsequent inhale, allow your belly to expand, bring in a little more breath so your lower chest rises, and then more air so your upper chest rises.
4. During the next deep inhale, allow your belly to expand, bring in a little more breath so your lower chest rises, bring in a little more breath so your upper chest rises, now open your throat so you are filled with breath from your nose down to your belly.

5. On a final deep inhale, allow your belly to expand, bring in a little more breath so your lower chest rises, bring in a little more breath so your upper chest rises, open your throat so you are filled with breath, and now exhale completely with purpose, energy, and the intention to let it all go.

Now relax into your natural breath. Allow your body to fully relax. Hang out here as long as you'd like, noticing how you are feeling physically and emotionally. Come back whenever you are ready. Take your time. Imagine there is no rush.

The Box Breath

A slight variation of the 5-Phase Breath, the Box Breath promotes relaxation and mental clarity. It involves inhaling deeply for a count of four, holding the breath for four, exhaling for four, and holding the breath again for four, all in a steady rhythm. This controlled pattern helps activate the parasympathetic nervous system, reducing stress and anxiety, while enhancing focus and concentration. Let's give it a try:

Begin with mindful preparation. Find a comfortable place to sit or lie down on your back. Let this place be warm, comfortable, safe, and free of distractions. Go ahead and get comfortable now.

1. Inhale through your nose four counts.
2. Hold the inhale four counts.
3. Exhale through your mouth four counts.
4. Hold the exhale four counts.
5. Repeat for a total of four cycles.

Now relax into your natural breath. Return to your natural breath and remain here as long as you'd like, noticing how you are feeling physically and emotionally. Come back whenever you are ready. Take your time. Imagine there is no rush.

Journal Prompts . . .

It's time to bring this home with some self-reflection exercises designed to elevate your awareness of your breathing and its impact on your daily life.

1. How have you noticed your breath influencing your mood and energy during different parts of your day? Write about any patterns you observe and consider how becoming more aware of your breathing could impact your overall well-being.
2. Think back to a recent time when you felt overwhelmed or stressed. How might practicing the 5-Phase Breath or the Box Breath have changed your experience in that moment? Describe how you could apply these breathing techniques to better manage similar situations in the future.

Bringing It All Together

In this chapter, you discovered that your breath is the vital thread that connects your heart, lungs, digestive system, nervous system, brain, thoughts, and spiritual consciousness.

The all-too-common shallow, unaware breath can be the culprit underlying many discomforts, including foggy brain, an inability to focus, confusion, heart palpitations, anxiety, panic attacks, depression, decreased vigor, and feelings of separation and loneliness. By becoming more mindful of your breath and intentionally expanding it, you'll likely notice a softening of these discomforts. The beauty of this practice lies in its accessibility—it requires minimal time, no financial investment, and carries no negative side effects. It's a painfree way to bring about profound changes in your physical, mental, emotional, and spiritual well-being.

While we are currently wrapping up our exploration of breath, know that we will return to its practice throughout your journey, as it is the most impactful foundation for developing mindfulness throughout your life. With this foundation firmly in place, we now dive in to how cultivating a beginner's mind—embracing curiosity and openness—enhances all things, including your journey from stressed to Zen!

THREE

THE BEGINNER'S MIND

EMBRACING CURIOSITY AND OPENNESS

In the beginner's mind, there are many possibilities;
in the expert's mind, there are few.

—SHUNRYU SUZIKI

The concept of "beginner's mind" originates from Zen Buddhism. It places a strong emphasis on learning with an open mind and having no preconceived notions— even when one is already proficient in the subject. Even if you are an expert, the aim is to approach work and life with the wonder and interest of a beginner.

Far too frequently, I've encountered individuals who exude an air of omniscience. You know the type—those who position themselves as authorities on numerous topics, implicitly conveying the message, "There's nothing you could tell me that I don't already know." Do you know anyone like this—a friend, family member, a professor, or maybe even yourself?

This mindset and way of presenting oneself often comes from a need to protect one's ego. The challenge is, such an approach sets a cap on personal growth and development—which results in not really knowing much at all. By acting like they know everything, people unknowingly block themselves from new insights and opportunities. While this attitude may provide a sense of security, it is also very limiting. In the end, this self-imposed limitation stifles curiosity, dampens creativity, and restricts the wide range of possibilities that come from having an open and receptive mind.

Imagine a young child playing at the beach for the first time. We will call her Evy. Every little thing captures her attention—the feel of the soft sand between her toes, the sparkle of seashells scattered along the shore, and the rhythmic sound of the waves crashing. With wide-eyed wonder, she picks up a seashell and, without any preconceived notions or judgments, examines its texture, color, and shape. She might find herself asking: "Why is this shell shiny? What's inside of it? How did it get here?"

In this moment, Evy embodies an open mind, embracing a sense of discovery and allowing herself to be fully present in the experience. She isn't constrained by previous knowledge or assumptions; instead, she is driven purely by curiosity and the desire to explore. This openness enables her to learn and grow in ways that a closed-off mindset would hinder.

Applying childlike curiosity and openness to your own life enables you to approach new experiences, tasks, and interactions with a sense of wonder and eagerness to learn.

This frees you from having a limited mindset and fosters continuous growth. By approaching even familiar situations with an open mind and a willingness to see things differently, you can find new and novel ways to experience them. This will allow you to continually learn, grow, and find joy in everyday experiences. Here are a few suggestions to practice greater curiosity and openness:

- Rewatch a movie for the second, third, or even fifth time with a beginner's mind. Allow yourself to see, feel, and experience the film from a fresh perspective each time. Remind yourself that you are not the same person who saw it the first time and remain open to discovering concepts, jokes, and characters that you may have missed.

- Return to a familiar hangout spot multiple times. With a beginner's mind, you can discover and connect with its land and people in new, enriching ways. Each visit offers fresh insights and experiences, as you remain open and receptive to what the place has to offer.

- Enter the same classroom where you've been sitting all semester with a fresh and inspiring mental invitation. Pay attention to details like the texture of the floor, the frames around the windows, and the way the light streams in. You have the power to transform a familiar space into a canvas full of new discoveries and perspectives.

When you approach such events with the mentality that "I have previously experienced this, thus I know it all," you severely limit your ability to view them with an open heart and mind. This narrow-eyed mindset prevents you from exploring new areas, or a greater depth within the concepts you believe you already know.

The Power of a Growth Mindset

In today's culture, the concept of the beginner's mind aligns closely with what is often referred to as a "growth mindset." Embracing a beginner's mind means fostering an attitude that welcomes continuous learning and personal development. It encourages you to lean in and embrace curiosity, seeing each moment as an opportunity to expand your understanding and capabilities. A growth mindset propels you forward, enabling you to tackle challenges with resilience and view setbacks as stepping stones rather than obstacles. Adopting this mindset requires the courage to step outside your comfort zone, acknowledge that you don't have all the answers, and be open to new perspectives and ideas. It means being willing to make mistakes and learn from them, rather than seeing them as failures. When you navigate life with a beginner's mind, you engage more deeply with each experience; foster richer, more meaningful connections; and unlock more of your limitless potential.

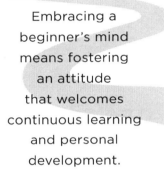

Embracing a beginner's mind means fostering an attitude that welcomes continuous learning and personal development.

The mind of the beginner is empty,
free of the habits of the expert, ready to accept,
to doubt, open to all possibilities.

SHUNRYU SUZUKI

As you advance on your mindfulness journey, embracing a beginner's mind will enrich your experiences by not only enhancing your learning, but also creating more fun and enjoyment along the way. To ensure you're set up for success, let's explore a few key foundations of the beginner's mind:

Enhanced Curiosity. Mindfulness thrives on curiosity. By keeping a beginner's mind, you approach each moment with wonder and eagerness to learn, allowing yourself to notice subtle details and nuances that you might otherwise overlook.

With this fresh perspective, even routine activities become fascinating explorations. For example, sipping a cup of tea can transform into a rich sensory experience where you appreciate the aroma, taste, and warmth in new ways. A simple walk can turn into an adventure where you observe the play of light through leaves, hear the varied sounds of nature, and feel the textures of the ground beneath your feet.

Enhanced curiosity also helps you become more aware of your internal experiences. You will notice patterns of thoughts, emotions, and physical sensations you may have previously ignored. This deeper level of attention can lead to greater self-understanding and therefore emotional balance.

When you bring this inquisitive mindset to your mindfulness practice, it keeps you engaged and prevents the routine from becoming monotonous. Instead of just going through the motions, you're actively exploring and learning from each moment.

An Open Mind. A beginner's mind cultivates a sense of openness, enabling you to approach each moment free from preconceived notions, biases, or judgments. This openness allows you to see things as they truly are, rather than through the lens of past experiences or expectations. By letting go of the mental filters that often cloud your perception, you become more attuned to the subtleties and richness of the present moment. This heightened awareness helps you fully engage with whatever you are experiencing, whether it's your breath, the sound of leaves rustling, or the energy of the crowd at a football game. Appreciating each moment in its entirety leads to a deeper understanding and a more profound connection with the world around you. It enables you to live more aware, savor the small details, and find joy in the ordinary, which can often be overlooked when your mind is cluttered with preconceived ideas and judgments.

With regard to keeping an open mind, consider this timeless parable:

> Once upon a time in a small village, there lived a farmer and his son. The farmer was well-respected and known for his wisdom and hard work. One day, the farmer's horse ran away. The neighbors came by to offer their condolences, saying, "What bad luck!" The farmer simply replied, "Maybe yes, maybe no. We shall see."
>
> A few days later, the horse returned, bringing with it several wild horses. The neighbors came by once more to congratulate the farmer, exclaiming, "What good fortune!" Again, the farmer replied, "Maybe yes, maybe no. We shall see."
>
> Shortly thereafter, the farmer's son attempted to ride one of the wild horses, but was thrown off and broke his leg. The neighbors hurried over to express their sympathy, lamenting, "What terrible luck!" The farmer once again replied calmly, "Maybe yes, maybe no. We shall see."
>
> A week passed, and a group of soldiers came to the village to conscript young men to fight in a war. Because of his broken leg, the farmer's son was not taken. The neighbors were amazed by the twist of fate and said, "What incredible luck!" The farmer, keeping to his consistent perspective, responded once more, "Maybe yes, maybe no. We shall see."

This parable encourages us to withhold judgment and remain open to the unfolding of events, recognizing that our initial reactions may not capture the full picture.

A Relaxed Ego. Adopting a beginner's mind helps you set aside ego-driven thoughts and the mistaken belief that you already know everything. This kind of humility encourages a learning attitude, making you more open to new insights and different perspectives.

When you let go of ego, you stop worrying about "proving" yourself or being right all of the time. Instead, you become more willing to listen to others, consider new ideas, and try out different experiences. This openness leads to more genuine interactions and deeper connections with others because you're not focused on protecting or promoting your self-image. It also provides ease and relaxation to the nervous system, which is on overdrive when you are constantly trying to persuade and prove your worthiness to yourself and others.

When practicing mindfulness, letting go of your ego allows you to approach life experiences with curiosity and a fresh perspective. You stop comparing yourself to others or to your past self, and therefore simply focus on the present moment. This openness helps you learn and grow from each experience, making your mindfulness journey richer and more fulfilling.

In my experience, college students often operate from a heightened state of ego . . . and it's easy to see why. They are frequently judged by their peers, professors, and employers, as well as by themselves. The ego acts as a protective mechanism, helping them stand out in a highly competitive environment. This makes it challenging to let down their guard and soften their ego.

However, the invitation here is to practice openness and curiosity. By cultivating these habits early, you set the stage for continued growth, fueling your future stages of development. These practices equip you to navigate life's challenges with greater resilience and insight, paving the way for a more enriching and fulfilling journey ahead.

I love talking with, and being around,
ego-driven, know-it-all people.

—NOBODY

Less Judgment. Having a beginner's mind helps you dial down judgment toward yourself, others, and your experience. When you approach things without those harsh, critical thoughts, you naturally reduce negative self-talk. This shift of perspective helps you to be kinder to yourself and others.

Imagine catching yourself in a mistake and instead of the usual, "I can't believe I did that, I'm so stupid," you think, "Well, that's interesting. What can I learn from this?" Suddenly, you're not beating yourself up, but growing from the experience.

This practice of nonjudgment makes you more compassionate toward yourself. You start treating yourself like you would a good friend, offering support and understanding instead of criticism. Over time, this fosters a healthier, more loving relationship with yourself and creates a more positive and encouraging inner dialogue. Less judgment means you give yourself the freedom to explore, make mistakes, and grow without the fear of harsh self-criticism holding you back.

Increased Patience. When you approach life with a beginner's mind, full of curiosity and openness, you naturally start developing more patience. Instead of rushing through experiences or getting frustrated when something doesn't go as planned, you see each moment as a chance to learn something new.

For example, if you're practicing mindfulness and your mind keeps wandering, a beginner's mind helps you see that this is not a failure, but an opportunity to understand yourself better. You think, "Oh, my mind wandered again. Interesting. Why is it wandering so much today? How can I bring more peace to my mind in this moment?" This way, instead of getting upset, which creates a negative downward spiral of thoughts and then emotions, you become more patient with yourself and the process, creating a positive upward spiral of thoughts and emotions.

By viewing each experience—no matter how small or challenging—as a valuable learning opportunity, you reduce the frustration and impatience that often come with practicing mindfulness. This shift in perspective helps you stay calm and collected, whether you are trying to meditate, dealing with stress, or facing a setback. Over time, this increased patience spills over into other areas of life, helping you handle everyday challenges with a lot more grace, understanding, and resilience.

Authentic Engagement. Embracing a beginner's mind encourages you to engage genuinely with your mindfulness journey. When you let go of the pressure to achieve or be perfect, you free yourself to simply experience things as they are. This openness helps you connect more deeply with the present moment in a real, unfiltered way.

Think about it. When you're not stressing about getting everything right or hitting some kind of "mindfulness milestone," you can actually enjoy the practice. You become less focused on the result (the outcome) and more on what's happening right now (the journey). This brings a sense of authenticity to each experience—whether you're sitting in meditation, walking through the park, or washing the dishes.

When you engage authentically, your interactions with others become richer and more meaningful. By letting go of the need to project a certain image or prove something, you can listen more intently and respond more thoughtfully. Instead of worrying about what to say next or how you're being perceived, you're fully present in the conversation. This genuine interest is felt by others, deepening your relationships and making them more fulfilling.

Imagine chatting with a friend and truly hearing them, not just waiting for your turn to speak. Picture spending time with family, fully engaged rather than distracted by your thoughts or scrolling through Instagram. This level of presence and authenticity helps fulfill the fundamental human desire to be seen and heard, leading to more supportive and rewarding connections.

In practice, and in life, cultivating a beginner's mind can enhance learning, creativity, and problem-solving abilities. It allows for fresh perspectives and can lead to deeper insights and more authentic experiences. This mindset is useful not only in meditation and contemplative practices, but in all aspects of life—from work, to relationships, to personal growth. It's a win-win that brings more joy, understanding, and depth to every area of your life.

Ways to Foster Curiosity and Openness

You might be wondering how you can become more curious and open-minded. Here are a few practices—along with some examples from other college students—to help you along your way:

🖋 **Approach Tasks with Wonder.** Even familiar tasks can be approached as if it's the first time. Notice details you might otherwise overlook.

Maddie, a student in my Meditation in the 21st Century course, frequently remarked, "I've been practicing meditation and attending yoga classes for years. I already know all of this." Unfortunately, this mindset significantly hindered her ability to learn and grow. It was as if she erected a barrier at every opportunity to gain new insights or deepen her practice, and as a result, she diminished her level of satisfaction and fulfillment in the class. Moreover, this attitude created a metaphorical armor around her, making it challenging for other students to connect with her.

🖋 **Ask Questions.** Instead of assuming you know the answers, ask questions and be genuinely curious about the answers you receive.

Remember Tyler? A refreshing and inspiring attribute about him was his willingness to stay after class to ask clarifying questions. He openly shared that he had a learning disorder, which sometimes made it challenging for him to follow the day's lessons. He was open-minded, fully listening to my response as if it was the first time he had heard it. He wrote notes and stayed engaged in the conversation throughout. Not only did I appreciate his willingness to ask questions, but he also gained a great deal of insight by having the courage to ask and the willingness to listen.

Embrace the Unknown. Be comfortable with not having all the answers, and consider the unknown as an opportunity for new adventures rather than a threat.

Antoni, a student at the University of Minnesota, secretly shared with me the anxiety he felt while facing the unknown. Due to a chaotic childhood, embracing uncertainty was a tremendous challenge for him. However, after learning about the beginner's mind and reminding himself that he is safe and able to welcome the unknown, he made a conscious effort to practice breathing and relaxation techniques when confronted with an uncertain future. This intentional approach helped him navigate his anxiety and cultivate greater resilience, which was especially valuable for him as he approached graduation and his subsequent job interviews.

Be Open to Feedback. Accept feedback and input from others, seeing it as a chance to grow and learn rather than a challenge to your competence.

Kaylin, a junior majoring in Environmental Science, was known around campus for their remarkable ability to accept feedback with grace and enthusiasm. Unlike many of their peers, who often recoiled at constructive criticism, Kaylin saw every piece of feedback as a valuable gift. Whether it was from their professors, classmates, or mentors, they listened attentively, asked thoughtful questions for clarification, and applied the insights with genuine eagerness. Their openness not only helped them excel academically, but also made them a respected member of group projects and a sought-after friend.

Let Go of Ego. Recognize that being an "expert" can sometimes limit your learning. Stay open and acknowledge that there's always something new to discover.

Melinda, a senior at CU Boulder, grew up in an environment where not knowing something felt unsafe. Her parents, both highly intelligent achievers, had set high expectations for her from an early age. This pressure to measure up to their intellectual standards led her to develop an overactive ego, creating a façade of constant competence. Admitting she didn't know something was exceptionally challenging for her, as she felt a relentless need to appear just as intelligent as her parents. This behavior pattern kept her in a box, unwilling to learn new things—about life, about others, and about herself.

Adopt a Growth Mindset (the Beginner's Mind). Focus on the potential for growth and improvement rather than on proving your abilities. Embrace challenges as opportunities to develop your skills, and focus on the process not the outcome.

Payton, a sophomore on the college track team, first encountered the concept of a beginner's mind in a high school health course and immediately connected with the idea of a growth mindset. He embraced the philosophy of letting go of outcomes while concentrating on the process. In both his track training and racing, Payton cultivated a mindset that focused intntly on the elements within his control, releasing any attachment to the outcome. He became acutely aware of the importance of not getting swept up in the results of his races, such as his finish times or whether he placed on the podium. This approach not only enhanced his performance, but also brought a sense of peace and fulfillment to his athletic journey and beyond.

Cultivate Playfulness. Allow yourself to experiment and play. Taking things less seriously can often lead to more innovative thinking and creative solutions.

Samantha, a junior in engineering, was renowned for her playful and lighthearted approach to life, all thanks to her embrace of the beginner's mind. Early on, Samantha discovered that she thought more clearly, engaged better with others, and enjoyed herself more when she was playful. To counterbalance the intense seriousness of her major, she intentionally enrolled in engaging courses such as acting, dancing, yoga, and drawing. She approached each of these courses with boundless curiosity, excitement, and a childlike sense of play. Samantha's infectious enthusiasm and open-minded attitude not only made her a standout engineering student, but also a cherished friend. She served as a constant reminder to her peers that even in the rigorous field of engineering, there is immense value in lightening up and finding joy through playfulness.

By embracing the beginner's mind, you can enrich your life with continuous learning and growth, all while experiencing a deeper, more engaged connection with the world around you. This perspective is essential as you embark on your own mindfulness journey, an endless, winding and imperfect adventure filled with practicing, living, experimenting, learning, laughing, settling, rising, and growing.

Let's Practice . . .

Savor a Hot Cup of Tea or Coffee

This exercise encourages you to prepare and drink your favorite beverage with a beginner's mind, paying attention to details you might usually overlook. Imagine you're new to this planet, exploring everything for the first time. Learn to use your hands and fingers, discover the cup, embrace its handle, and bring it to your mouth playfully and curiously. Get playful and have fun with this fresh perspective.

Mindfully prepare your beverage. Choose your favorite tea or coffee and prepare it mindfully. Turn off other distractions such as the TV, radio, and your phone. Notice the process of boiling the water, measuring the tea leaves or coffee grounds, choosing your favorite mug, then pouring the hot water. Pay attention to the sounds, smells, and movements.

Find a comfortable space. Settle into a comfortable spot where you can sit quietly undisturbed. Hold your cup in your hands, feel its warmth, smell the aroma, notice your emotions—all of them.

Set an intention. Take a few deep breaths to center yourself. Set an intention to approach this experience with curiosity and openness, as if you are drinking this tea or coffee for the very first time.

Observe the visuals. Look at your beverage carefully. Notice the color, the rising steam, and the way the liquid moves in the cup. Observe the subtle details and variations in color or texture.

Engage your sense of smell. Bring the cup close to your nose and take a deep, slow inhale. Notice the aroma. What specific scents can you detect? Is there a difference in the intensity of the aroma at varying distances? Try to appreciate the complexity and richness of the smell.

Feel the temperature. Hold the cup in both hands and feel its warmth. Notice the sensation of heat radiating through the cup into your palms and fingers. How does the temperature shift over time as the liquid cools?

Listen to the sounds. As you lift the cup and take a sip, pay attention to any sounds. The gentle clink of the cup against the table, the soft slurp as you take a sip, and the subtle swish of the liquid in your mouth. Notice how these sounds change with each action.

Taste with awareness. Take a small sip and let the liquid sit on your tongue. Notice the initial flavors and how they evolve. What is the texture like? Is it smooth, creamy, or perhaps slightly gritty? Swallow slowly and observe the aftertaste. Pay attention to how the flavors change and linger in your mouth.

Feel the sensations. As you take a sip, pay attention to the texture and temperature of the liquid in your mouth. Is it smooth, thick, or thin? Notice how it feels as you swallow, as well as the sensations it leaves behind.

Reflect on the experience. After a few minutes of mindful sipping, take a moment to reflect on the experience. How did it feel to drink your tea or coffee with such detailed attention? What new discoveries did you make about an otherwise routine activity?

Integrate these practices into other daily routines. Consider how you can bring this level of mindful attention to other activities, such as getting ready in the morning, studying, walking, driving, communicating, and winding down at night. How might this exercise influence the way you approach other aspects of your life?

Journal Prompts . . .

1. **Describe Your Experience:** Something I noticed about the look, smell, and taste of my tea or coffee is . . .
2. **Emotional Response:** Some emotions and thoughts that came up for me during this practice is/are . . . Something that surprised me was . . . Paying close attention to this simple practice affected my mood by . . .
3. **Challenges and Growth:** A challenge (wandering mind, judgment, feeling rushed, etc.) that I encountered during the practice was . . . I addressed it by . . .

4. Personal Insights: Some new personal insights or realizations that emerged are . . . How this practice might influence my overall approach to my mindfulness journey is . . .

Bringing It All Together

In summary, embodying a beginner's mind means approaching life with a sense of wonder, humility, and an openness to learning. By adopting this mindset, you continually enrich your understanding, deepen your experiences, and maintain a flexible, dynamic approach to life's challenges and opportunities. It allows you to let down your guard and practice acceptance of the unknown without feeling the need to have all the answers. You get to play, embrace childlike curiosity, and savor the joy of discovery. The beginner's mind fosters ease, patience, and acceptance—creating a life characterized by peace and fulfillment—that together contribute to a comforting and empowering foundation for your mindfulness journey.

Next, we explore another key foundation for your mindfulness journey—what I call "embracing the precious present." By immersing yourself in the present moment, you give your mind permission to let go of past regrets and future anxieties, and find power in the now. Let's explore how fully embracing the present can further enhance all of your moments.

FOUR

THE PRECIOUS PRESENT

FINDING POWER IN THE NOW

*The past is gone, the future is not yet here,
and if we do not go back to ourselves in the present moment,
we cannot be in touch with life.*

—THICH NHAT HANH

On the University of Wisconsin, Milwaukee (UWM) campus, life moved at a dizzying pace. Students and professors scurried about in a hurry to get somewhere. Amidst the frenzy, Tyler, a UWM college student, found himself swirling with overwhelm, confusion, and anxiety.

Tyler's mind was racing with ideas about his life as he made his way across campus. His days were occupied with classes, homework, and part-time work. He spent forty-five minutes, each way, on the public bus because he lived off campus in a challenging area of the city. He had to plan his next move three steps ahead of time. "Which bus should I board to arrive at class on time?" "What should I pack for my day and for my job after class so that I am prepared for all of it?" "Do I have what it takes to succeed?" "Did I support my friend well enough last week?" He was overcome with concerns for both the past and the future. His existence was a never-ending loop of worry and anxiety.

While he was navigating this jumble of thoughts and emotions, he turned to his phone, hoping that scrolling social media while he walked would provide distraction from his worries. One block from his class, he stepped off the curb to cross the road. So wrapped up in his thoughts, he didn't realize he was crossing during a "do not walk" cycle. A car sped toward him, hitting him with its side mirror and knocking him to the ground. Tyler hit the pavement with such force, his backpack, phone, and shoes flew away from him. Stunned, he lay there for several minutes, trying to catch his breath and make sense of what had just happened.

To his dismay, no one came to assist him, and the car did not slow down to check on him, the driver diverted by his own thoughts and hectic life. Tyler got up slowly, gathered his things, and moved cautiously toward a nearby bench so he could take a breather. As he calmed his nervous system, it hit him loud and clear: "I need to change something in my life. This way of thinking and being is dangerous!"

The next day Tyler received an unexpected call from his old friend, Sam. They had grown up together, and Sam, much like an older brother, had always been Tyler's source of wisdom and calm. Sam asked if he'd like to meet at Lincoln Park, a green oasis in the heart of the city, for a much-needed catch-up. Feeling compelled to see his wise friend, especially after yesterday's incident, Tyler took time off from his busy schedule and headed to the park. As he walked through the park's winding paths, flanked by towering trees with leaves in a kaleidoscope of vibrant fall colors, he felt a sense of peace begin to wash over him.

Upon arriving, Tyler found Sam sitting on a bench near a small pond, where ducks paddled lazily and the water reflected the clear blue sky above. Sam greeted Tyler with a warm, welcoming smile and their old secret handshake. "Tyler, my friend, it's been too long," Sam said, his voice calm and steady. At the sound of Sam's voice and the feeling of his presence, Tyler felt his neck relax, his shoulders dropped, and he let out an audible sigh. As he and Sam caught up on old times and shared stories from their recent experiences, Tyler finally spilled everything he had been bottling up inside.

"Sam, I'm at a loss about what to do with my life lately. I've been feeling incredibly overwhelmed—like, all the time. I'm constantly anxious about what's coming next and then ruminating over past mistakes. I desperately want to improve my situation, but it feels like I'm drowning in my own efforts. Just yesterday, I was so distracted by my thoughts that I even got hit by a car while crossing the street. I'm okay, but now my phone's broken, I missed all my classes, and I'm stuck in this seemingly endless cycle of negative thinking. It's like I'm trapped in a bad habit that I just can't break," he confessed, his head held low and his voice trembling.

"I'm scared," Tyler finally admitted. "I'm afraid if I don't do something soon, I might not make it through the semester."

Sam, resonating with Tyler's frustration, took a deep breath and allowed for a silent pause. During this pause, he noticed an elderly woman feeding ducks nearby; she was with a young boy who burst into laughter each time a duck waddled closer.

Intrigued by the excitement of the young boy, Sam nudged Tyler with his elbow and gestured toward the woman and child. Tyler glanced up and saw the pair, their loud laughter now fully breaking through his consciousness. At that moment, he realized he had been dimly aware of their laughter all along, but his preoccupations had kept him from truly absorbing it. Suddenly, his shoulders relaxed, and his breath deepened as a sense of calm began to wash over him. Sam reached into his pocket and handed Tyler some duck food, inviting him to walk toward the pond to feed the ducks. As Tyler focused on the water, the ducks, and the sound of the young boy's laughter, he noticed his mindset and mood state shifting. His worries faded into ease. His fear shifted into joy. He was returning to the present moment.

The ducks splashed and quacked, the boy laughed, and the elderly woman smiled kindly at them. In that simple shared moment, Tyler felt "the connection"—the connection with nature, with beauty, and with people; one whom he knew and the other two strangers. He was surprised he could feel this kind of connection in such a short period with a place and people he was unfamiliar with. The peace and joy he felt in this moment was exactly what had been missing from his busy life.

Once the duck food was gone, Tyler and Sam sat back on their bench. "You know, Tyler," Sam started, "the most profound joys often come from the simplest moments. Feeding the ducks, sharing laughter, being with friends—these things help us feel grounded and recharged. But you have to be present to appreciate them. In this busy world of ours, it takes awareness, patience, and practice to live in the present moment—but it isn't only doable; it is absolutely worth the effort."

What Keeps You from the Precious Present?

Over the years of working with students, I've discovered common themes that pull and tug at us, keeping us from experiencing—let alone relishing—the present. The tendency to avoid living in the present moment can be attributed to various psychological, societal, and personal factors. Here are ten of the most common reasons people struggle with staying present:

1. Fear and Anxiety

- **Future Worries:** Many people are preoccupied with concerns about the future, such as career, finances, relationships, and health, which often leads to anxiety and distracts from the goodness of the present. This is especially prevalent with college students, as their focus is generally on graduating, securing a good job, and building a meaningful life—all somewhere in the future.

- **Fear of the Unknown:** The future is uncertain, and this uncertainty can often lead to worry and mental projection. The truth is that nothing in life is truly certain—certainty itself is an illusion. Why not live in the now, where you have the greatest potential to fully experience life and make meaningful decisions?

2. Regret or Longing

- **Unresolved Issues:** Dwelling on past mistakes, failures, or traumatic events can prevent a person from focusing on the present.

- **Nostalgia:** Longing for "better days" or reminiscing about past experiences can also pull attention away from current realities.

3. Societal Pressures

- **FOMO (Fear of Missing Out):** Society often emphasizes future goals, achievements, and milestones, pressuring individuals to constantly plan and strive for more rather than appreciating the present.

- **Value for Busyness:** Modern life is fast-paced, with an emphasis on productivity and multitasking, which can make it difficult to slow down and savor the current moment. People like to compare how busy they are with

others, as if the busier—and therefore more frazzled—
they are, the more worthy they are. People have come
to wear their busyness as a badge of honor.

4. Technology and Distractions

- **Digital Overload:** The constant influx of notifications, social media updates, and digital entertainment can fragment attention and make it hard to
focus on the present.

- **Escapism:** Many people use technology as a way to
escape from their immediate reality, which can divert
attention from experiencing the here and now.

5. Lack of Mindfulness

- **Unawareness:** Some individuals are not aware of the
concept of mindfulness or do not practice it regularly,
which means they lack the skills to remain present—much
like Tyler stepping off the curb into an oncoming car.

- **Habitual Thinking:** Poor thought habits can include
thinking the same mindless things over and over.
People can develop mind-wandering and daydreaming
habits that become a default mode of operation, taking
them away from the present.

6. Emotional Avoidance

- **Intense Emotions:** The present moment can sometimes be challenging or painful. To avoid discomfort,
people might retreat into thinking about the past
or future.

- **Stress and Trauma:** Individuals who have experienced significant stress or trauma might find it difficult to stay present due to the emotional weight they carry.

7. Cognitive Conditioning

- **Planning and Problem-Solving:** From a young age, we are taught to plan ahead and solve problems. While these skills are valuable, they can condition the mind to always be focused on what's next rather than what's now.

- **Cultural Norms:** In many cultures, there's an emphasis on success, progress, and moving forward, which can detract from an appreciation of the present.

8. Overwhelm and Burnout

- **Information Overload:** The sheer amount of infor-mation and responsibilities people juggle daily can lead to mental fatigue, making it difficult to stay grounded in the present moment.

- **Chronic Stress:** Constant stress can put the brain in a state of hypervigilance, always anticipating the next issue or challenge.

9. Lack of Gratitude

- **Taking Things for Granted:** People may overlook the small joys and blessings in their everyday lives because they take them for granted or are constantly seeking something more or better.

- **Comparisons:** Regularly comparing oneself to others can create dissatisfaction with the present, pushing focus toward future achievements or past shortcomings.

10. Unmet Expectations

- **Unrealistic Standards:** Setting high or unrealistic expectations for oneself can lead to perpetual dissatisfaction, as the present moment often falls short of these ideals.

- **Perfectionism:** Striving for perfection can cause individuals to miss out on the beauty of the imperfect present, always aiming for what it could be rather than appreciating what it is.

> Success is important, but only if you are present enough to experience the satisfaction of those often-fleeting moments.

Understanding the various issues at play can be a crucial first step in cultivating greater mindfulness and presence in daily life. By recognizing the factors that pull you away from the present, you can take intentional steps to counteract them, such as a daily mindfulness practice, setting aside time for reflection, developing habits that encourage present-moment awareness, and choosing moments like sitting by a pond feeding the ducks.

The irony is that by constantly striving for success and adhering to a culture of perpetual busyness, you often miss out on the very essence of what it means to live fully. You sacrifice the simple joys and moments of peace that bring true fulfillment and happiness. These precious present moments are where life happens, where connections are made, and where your sense of purpose and well-being reside.

When you allow yourself to slow down and be fully present, you become more in tune with your surroundings and with yourself. This presence enables you to respond to life's demands more effectively because you are coming from a place of balance and clarity rather than fatigue and stress.

The Gifts of the Present

In a life where we have normalized the "squirrel mentality"— the tendency to be easily distracted, darting from one task to another, and lacking deep focus, we often miss the price-less gifts of the present moment. The "precious present" of-fers genuine joy, deep connection, and peace that can't be scheduled. Embracing the now lets us fully engage with life, savoring the simple moments that mean the most.

When you embrace the present, you:

- **Rediscover Joy:** Small pleasures—like a warm cup of tea, a gentle breeze, or a kind smile—become sources of happiness and contentment.
- **Enhance Relationships:** Being fully present with others fosters deeper connections and more meaningful interactions, whether with a loved one, a classmate, or the grocery store clerk.
- **Increase Productivity:** Paradoxically, taking regular breaks and being present enhances your focus and efficiency whenever you need to work hard.
- **Improve Health:** Reduced stress and greater emotional balance contribute to better physical and mental health.
- **Establish Clarity:** Presence allows you to clearly see your priorities and make decisions that align with your true values and desires.

In essence, living in the present is not about renounc-ing ambition or effort, contrary to some people's fears; it's about allowing yourself to be engaged in the moment, hearing the words someone is sharing, feeling your emo-tions while watching a movie, smelling the bacon while it is cooking, taking in your surroundings while walking to class, and having the awareness to experience harmony in any given moment. It is about realizing that genuine fulfillment and success result from living each moment to the fullest rather than from a never-ending, multitask-ing grind. Success is important, but only if you are present enough to experience the satisfaction of those often-fleet-ing moments.

When I turn down the volume, it's amazing how much I can actually hear.

JOHN WAIRE

Melinda, a student in my Mind Body Awareness course, arrived to class giddy with excitement, clearly eager to share something with all her classmates. The week before this class, I had given them the assignment to practice being more mindful of the moments; to pay closer attention to what they were experiencing by decreasing distractions and permitting themselves to heighten their awareness of the present.

Today, when I asked the class how this experiential assignment went, Melinda was the first to shoot up her hand. She was practically bouncing in her seat, super excited to share her experience:

> Last week, I thought this assignment was kind of silly. I figured I was already pretty aware of the present moment. But I decided to give it a shot. Yesterday, while I was on the bus to campus, I put down my phone and put away my earbuds. I took three deep breaths and just started paying attention to everything around me.
>
> I noticed people who, now that I'm thinking about it, I see every day on this bus. I noticed that the seats are green—who knew? I saw the bus driver, took in the smell of the bus, and watched how the windows moved up and down like they did on my old high school bus. And then, I saw something that completely blew my mind: the lake. Lake Michigan!
>
> It hit me—this was the first time I'd noticed this massive lake we drive next to every single day. This huge, 321-by-118-mile lake [22,000 square miles] appeared as if out of nowhere. For an entire year, I've been parking my car in the lot by the lake, riding the bus along its shore, and I never noticed it. I suddenly felt lit up inside with this discovery, but also kind of embarrassed. Here I was, thinking I was all "in the moment," and now needed to admit that I have been totally unaware.

I was astounded by how much I had been missing. That one bus ride completely changed my perspective. It made me realize just how important it is to be genuinely present, not just going through the motions. From now on, I'm going to make it a point to really see and appreciate the world around me—including that incredible lake right next door.

In a society that demands quick success, nonstop work, and constant multitasking, it may seem counterintuitive or even unproductive to slow down, breathe deeply, and create intentional space in your day. However, the truth remains that you are at your most powerful when you are fully present and attentive to yourself and those around you. Remember, the past is behind you and cannot be changed, and the future has yet to unfold, lying beyond your control. But the present—the now—is here, right in front of you, and this is where your greatest power resides. By paying attention to what is happening within you and around you, you not only elevate your current experience, but your also enhance your ability to influence the moments that follow.

Let's Practice . . .

Let's practice two simple yet very impact-filled practices—walking and talking (listening, really). It doesn't take any extra time; it is simply you doing something you are already doing—walking and talking. These exercises aim to help you savor the richness of the present moment and deepen your everyday experiences.

1. **Present Walking.** Practice being in the moment while walking around campus. Place your phone

in your backpack where it is hard to reach so you are not tempted to multitask while walking.

- Connect with your breath feeling the inhale and exhale as you are moving.
- Observe your five senses and notice five things you see, five things you hear, five things you smell, five things you taste, five things you feel kinesthetically——i.e. the breeze through your hair, the sun on your face; etc., and five things you feel emotionally.
- Allow yourself to observe without judgment; simply notice.
- Notice how this brings you into the present moment, where there is no room for anxiety of the future or worry about the past. Even if you can only hold this feeling for a minute or two, there is no judgment, just practice.

2. **Present Talking.** Practice listening and sharing conversation while being present in the moment.

- While conversing with someone, take a deep breath and give yourself permission to listen, really listen. When your attention begins drifting away, take a deep breath, bringing yourself back to the present moment. Often the mind begins thinking about how to respond, but in this preoccupation, much is missed. Allow the other person to fully share while you remain fully present.
- Practice being fully present in your next conversation. Listen attentively to the person speaking, notice their facial expressions, and truly engage with what they are saying. When they have finished, follow up with a question or comment that engages the conversation, resulting in them feeling seen and heard.

Journal Prompts . . .

1. I live more in the past/present/future . . . An example of this is . . .
2. A time when I felt fully present was . . . I was doing . . . and this made me feel . . .
3. Write about an experience or a time in your life when you were unaware, like Melinda in the story above. Write everything about it, including the outcome.
4. Write about an experience or time in your life when you were very present and aware of everything going on within you and around you. What was this like, and what was the outcome?

Bringing It All Together

In a world that not only normalizes squirrel mentality, but also often glorifies busyness, constant striving, and multitasking, the power of living in the moment might feel wrong, as if you are not doing enough because you don't feel stressed, anxious, or worried. To go unconscious in the moment by engaging in distractions is easy and common; many around you do it, making it feel normal, accepted, and even celebrated. However, the truth is that you miss many meaningful and delicious opportunities to experience the fullness of life all around you and within you. By focusing on your breath, engaging your senses, and finding gratitude in the present, you unlock a deeper connection to yourself and your surroundings. This present awareness allows you to navigate distractions with grace, appreciate simple joys, and respond to life's challenges with clarity and resilience. As you cultivate this practice, you will not only enhance your emotional well-being, but you will rediscover the true essence of living fully. Embracing the present moment enriches your experiences, strengthens your relationships, and ultimately leads you to a more meaningful, fulfilled, and aligned life.

Now that you're practicing conscious breathing, embracing a beginner's mind, and harnessing the power of the present moment, you'll find it easier to heighten your awareness of your entire being. By tapping in to the beauty and wisdom of your whole integrated Self—physical, mental, emotional, and spiritual—you will begin to recognize and appreciate the significance of each aspect as they contribute to the wholeness of who you are.

FIVE

THE WHOLISTIC PARADIGM

PHYSICAL, MENTAL, EMOTIONAL, AND SPIRITUAL ALIGNMENT

The whole is greater than the sum of its parts.

—ARISTOTLE

O nce upon a time in a village, there lived four blind men. The villagers told them, "There is an elephant in the village today." None of the blind men knew what an elephant was, so they decided, "Even though we cannot see it, let us go and feel it."

They went to the elephant, and each began to touch a different part of the large animal.

The first man touched the elephant's sturdy side and declared, "An elephant is like a wall."

The second man, feeling one of the tusks, said, "It is sharp and smooth. An elephant must be like a spear." Another rubbed its massive leg and concluded, "It is like a mighty tree." The fourth touched the elephant's large ear and said, "You are all mistaken. It is like a big fan."

They began to argue, each of them stoutly holding on to their own perspective. A wise man passing by saw the commotion and asked what they were arguing about. They told him, and the wise man said, "Each of you is right. The reason every one of you is telling it differently is because each of you has touched a different part of the elephant. The elephant has all those features, but to understand what an elephant truly is, you need to put all the parts together."

The blind men paused, and their arguments ceased. They realized that there was valuable truth in each of their perceptions, but that the complete reality required engaging with more than just one aspect.

The main takeaway here is that we can only get the full truth by looking at the entire picture and immersing ourselves in all its parts, not just focusing on isolated bits. Think about your own life—you need to attend to your physical sensations, thoughts, emotions, and spirit. Each plays a unique role, but it's in their interaction, where each part supports the others, that adds real depth and richness to your life. This concept of interconnectedness is what the wholistic paradigm is all about, helping you see the profound unity that ties together all the different aspects of your life.

Wholistic Paradigm—What Is It?

Wholistic" (sometimes spelled holistic") is defined by the *Merriam-Webster dictionary* as "dealing with the whole of something or someone, not just a part."[1] Basically, it's recognizing that there is always an interrelated/interdependent, symbiotic relationship at work. In other words, the whole is more than the sum

of its parts. To really get a handle on something, you have to understand how all the related pieces connect and interact.

The word *paradigm*," as defined by *Merriam-Webster*, is
"a philosophical and theoretical framework of a scientific school or discipline within which theories, laws, and generalizations are made."[2]

Putting it all together, a *Wholistic Paradigm* is a way of thinking that
appreciates the entire scope of who you are, including your physical,
mental, emotional, and spiritual aspects. The whole is only as strong
as its weakest link; therefore it is essential to increase the strength of all
aspects for the sake of the whole. Think of it as "nobody is left behind."

Your Four Bodies

In our work together, we'll refer to each individual aspect of the Self
as a "body." While most people typically think of the body as only the
physical aspect, our approach recognizes four distinct "bodies" that make
up who you are. We'll explore how this integrated perspective can lead
to a fuller understanding of well-being and personal growth. But before
we do, let's zoom in and explore each individual body in more detail.

1. Your Physical Body

Your physical body is the most straightforward to understand,
as it typically comes to mind when we mention the word *body*. It is the
tangible, biological entity composed of bones, muscles, organs, and
tissues—a structure you can touch and feel. Describing sensations
in the physical body is familiar and direct. For instance, when you
attune to your physical body, you might identify sensations such as:

- I feel energized.
- I have a headache.
- I feel hungry.
- I have a pain in my leg.
- I am tired.

The physical body is an extraordinary, resilient vessel that houses all
other aspects of your being. Despite its remarkable capacity for creativity

and regeneration, it is often subjected to neglect—lacking sufficient sleep, adequate movement, and proper nutrition, while enduring the weight of self-criticism over its size, shape, or ability. Yet, astonishingly, it continues to perform and heal, renewing itself from your very first breath to your last.

When we think about the physical body, it's easy to get distracted by society's obsession with appearance. We're bombarded with images and messages that prioritize looks over function, often neglecting the true essence of physical health. However, embracing a wholistic view means shifting our focus toward physical health, energy, performance, strength, and well-being. It's about nourishing our bodies with healthy foods, engaging in regular exercise, and listening to what our bodies need, and don't need. By doing so, we foster a stronger, more resilient physical self that supports us in all areas of our lives, rather than merely striving to meet superficial standards.

> The physical body is an extraordinary, resilient vessel that houses all other aspects of your being.

Check In: Pause. Take a deep 5-Phase Breath. Take a moment right now to stop reading and tune in to your physical body. Notice what you are experiencing, without judgment or expectation. No sensation is too small to identify. You might notice the position of your neck or the focus of your eyes or the feeling of this book in your hands. Once you've attached words to your sensations, document them in the margins or in your journal. This practice elevates your awareness and crystallizes your experience into words.

A healthy outside starts from the inside.

ROBERT URICH

2. Your Mental Body

Your mental body encompasses your thoughts, cognition, and judgment. It includes memories of the past, anticipations of the future, and awareness of the present moment. This aspect of yourself holds your beliefs, understandings, and the judgments you make about yourself and others. It also contains behavioral patterns established early in life that continue to shape your actions, either constructively or destructively, throughout your lifetime.

The mental body is the warehouse of your to-do lists and the *should haves* and *should not haves*. It houses your attitudes and perceptions. Contrary to popular belief, your mental body is fully within your control; however, many people fall into unconscious patterns, not fully embracing control of their thoughts.

Western society places considerable emphasis on the mental body, particularly in the realm of cognition, or what we often call "smarts." As a college student, you are immersed in a multi-year program designed to enhance your knowledge, sharpen your intellect, and advance your life through critical thinking. Our culture highly values education and academic achievement, viewing them as key indicators of success.

In the professional world, there's also tremendous focus placed on analytical problem-solving. Productivity, efficiency, and measurable outcomes often depend on cognitive abilities. From standardized tests and academic awards to job performance metrics and ongoing professional development, the spotlight is mostly on intellectual achievements, often ignoring emotional, physical, and spiritual well-being. This reinforces the idea that success is all about being "smart," downplaying the importance of other vital aspects of a balanced life.

Check In: Pause. Take a deep 5-Phase Breath. Go inside and notice what is taking up space in your mind. What are you thinking? You might even be aware of judgments regarding the content you just read. You might notice your mind thinking about your to-do lists or bouncing around to different memories. Once you are aware of your thoughts, record them in the margin or in your journal.

3. Your Emotional Body

Often, in literature and in practice, the emotional body is linked together tightly with the mental body, but this could not be more inaccurate. Your emotional body contains your emotions or feelings. They often feel illogical, contrary to the more logical leanings of the mental body. Your emotional body, when allowed to live fully, acts as an internal GPS system, providing you with feedback about all thoughts, decisions, and actions. Unfortunately, Western society often perpetuates negative messages about emotions, which further impedes emotional health and self-acceptance. Here are five such messages:

1. **Emotions are a sign of weakness.** Society often labels the expression of emotions, particularly sadness and fear, as a sign of weakness. This can lead individuals to suppress their emotional experiences and avoid showing and sharing vulnerability.

2. **Emotions should be controlled.** There's a prevalent belief that emotions need to be tightly controlled or even eliminated, suggesting that rationality and logic (the mental body) should dominate over emotional responses (feelings). This creates pressure to "keep it together" and not let emotions interfere with daily (or rational) life.

3. **There are positive and negative emotions.** Emotions are commonly referred to as either "positive" (good) or "negative" (bad). Feeling happy, joyful, and grateful are examples of common "good" emotions, while feeling angry, jealous, and sad are often deemed negative and therefore inappropriate to express. The truth is, *all* emotions are valuable, meaningful, and important. Tuning into your emotions and allowing them to act as your internal GPS will become your greatest superpower when you accept and embrace the full spectrum of your feelings.

4. **Men and women should feel and express emotions differently.** Traditional gender norms frequently impose the expectation that men should remain stoic and unemotional, discouraging them from openly expressing their feelings. This harmful stereotype perpetuates the notion that "real men"

don't cry or exhibit sensitivity, leading to emotional suppression. On the opposite end, women are often generalized as being more emotional—sometimes described as overly emotional. They face societal pressure to avoid expressing anger and to always act pleasant and accommodating. These stereotypical expectations create significant barriers to building a healthy and authentic connection with one's emotional body, regardless of gender.

5. **Emotions complicate decision-making.** Emotions are often seen as disruptions to logical and effective decision-making. This message implies that emotional input is inferior to rational thought, ignoring the valuable insights emotions can provide. These negative messages can suppress emotional health and authenticity, making it crucial to challenge and reframe them to support a more balanced and accepting view of human emotion.

Can you see how this negative messaging can impede your ability to connect full-heartedly with your feelings? I'm inviting you to debunk these limiting messages and begin creating an elevated relationship with your emotional body, one of great connection, beauty, and full-on feeling. The first step to accomplishing this is to more fully understand the primary types of emotion. Although many will say we have hundreds of emotions, the truth of the matter is we have four main emotions: mad, sad, glad, and scared. All other emotional descriptors are either synonyms of one of these four emotions, or are words that describe combinations of emotions.

You might be surprised to learn that you are always feeling *at least one* emotion in any given moment, and often more than one, sometimes even all four of them—yes, all at the same time.

That can seem confusing and complicated, but when you slow down, check in, and get honest with yourself, it can be easy and empowering to identify which emotions are currently taking up space. Let's take a look at a few examples:

Frustrated: This could be a combination of angry and scared.

Excited: *Excited* is a synonym for *glad*.

Anxious: This could be a combination of scared and glad, or it could be a combination of scared and sad.

I encourage you to slow down, check in, and identify what you are feeling. You don't need to ponder *why* you are feeling a certain way, as there is plenty of time for that. For now, simply open the portal to your feelings in a new and expansive way so you can make friends with your emotions again, without judgment.

Check In: Pause. Take a deep 5-Phase Breath. Give yourself permission to get honest and vulnerable with yourself. As,k "What am I feeling right now?" Let go of any expectations, judgments, or desires to understand *why* you're feeling a certain emotion. Simply check in. Use this format to help you clarify:

- Am I feeling mad?
- Am I feeling sad?
- Am I feeling glad?
- Am I feeling scared?

Once you feel ready, take a moment to jot down the emotions you've identified, either in the margins of this book or in your journal. Remember, at this stage, you don't need to understand the reasons behind these emotions. The focus is on practicing honesty with yourself by bravely tuning in to your feelings. The key to clearly identifying your emotions is to let go of judgment, expectation, and the need for explanations (which is an example of defaulting to the mental body, i.e., thoughts or judgment).

4. Your Spiritual Body

The spiritual body can be defined as the aspect of yourself that seeks connection, meaning, and purpose beyond the tangible world. It encompasses your sense of inner peace, your personal beliefs about the nature of existence, and your connection to something greater than yourself, whether that is the universe, nature, or a collective human experience. The spiritual body is nurtured through practices that include introspection, mindfulness, and a deep sense of connectedness with life and others.

The essence of the spiritual body includes:

- Cultivating inner harmony by building a sense of inner peace and balance.
- Connecting with purpose and meaning by exploring and understanding the deeper and wider purposes of life.
- Building relationships with the world around you by connecting with nature, art, community, and fostering personal introspection and a connection with others.
- Embracing personal growth by engaging in practices that promote self-awareness, such as meditation, self-reflection, or spending time outdoors.

Many of my students and clients have often shared that they have difficulty finding words to describe what they are experiencing in their spiritual body. This challenge is quite common, as the spiritual aspect of our being is often the least concrete and the most abstract. Unlike physical sensations or emotions, spiritual experiences can be subtle and deeply personal, making them harder to articulate. Moreover, in a world that frequently prioritizes material success and tangible results, spiritual well-being can be undervalued and misunderstood. This lack of societal focus on spiritual health can leave individuals feeling isolated or unsure when grappling with spiritual questions.

In addition, a lot of people mix spirituality with religion. If you've had good experiences with religion, that can be a solid base. But if your past with religion hasn't been great, it can shut you off from exploring your spirituality at all. Rather than avoid your spiritual self altogether, release what didn't work and find what does. Spirituality is much broader and deeper than any organized religion. This mix-up can get in the way of you finding deeper peace, meaning, and connection. If we can look at spirituality outside the confines of religion, it unveils many other avenues, like meditation, mindfulness, or even spending time in nature—anything that helps you connect with your inner self. By exploring these, you can find a spirituality that adds genuine richness to your life. A student of mine once commented, "With the falling apart of our spiritual communities, and the lack of something to take its place, I feel somewhat lost and confused with spirituality and what it truly is."

Check In: Pause. Take a deep 5-Phase Breath. Give yourself permission to go inside and connect with your spiritual body. What do you notice? Perhaps you notice connection, love, absence, isolation, harmony, expansiveness, peace, centeredness, or scatteredness. Once you feel ready, take a moment to record your insights in the margin or in your journal. As before, complete this check-in without judgment or expectation. Engage a beginner's mind as you explore and reflect with curiosity.

So, you might be wondering, "What's the deal with this wholistic paradigm? What's the point? Why should I care?" Well, here's the thing: When you pay attention to and honor all parts of yourself—your physical, mental, emotional, and spiritual bodies—you elevate your ability to thrive in every aspect of your life; you are living wholistically—with your whole self, rather than relying on just your thoughts or just your body. You become attuned to what your physical body needs, you guide your thoughts in ways that truly serve you, you embrace and respond to the inner guidance of your emotions, and you nurture a deep spiritual connection that brings inner peace. This, my friends, is the sweet spot of alignment.

Every thought, decision, and action taken from a place of alignment contributes to a more harmonious, effective, and fulfilling life. Here is where you can navigate challenges with greater clarity and embrace opportunities with confidence, because you're taking into consideration how the body feels, what your thoughts are, which emotions are created, and whether it is in alignment with your spirit.

Wellness is the complete integration of mind, body, heart and soul—the realization that everything we do, think, feel and believe as an effect on our state of well being.

GREG ANDERSON

Meet Alex, a student from my course, Meditation in the 21st Century. With an enviable intellect and a GPA to match, he was the person everyone turned to for help with complex equations and theories. But beneath this facade of academic brilliance, Alex was struggling.

Driven by his mental prowess, Alex lived almost entirely in his mind, viewing emotions and spirituality as distractions, trivial compared to the rigors of academia. He ran on coffee and late-night study sessions, priding himself on his ability to push through exhaustion for the sake of intellectual achievement. Emotions? Alex saw them as weaknesses, quickly brushing off any feelings that surfaced. Spirituality? He often scoffed at the idea, deeming it irrelevant in a world governed by logic and reason.

Over time, however, Alex began to notice cracks in his meticulously constructed life. He felt increasingly isolated, unable to connect with his peers on a deeper level. Social events felt more like obligations than opportunities for joy, and he found himself feeling inexplicably empty, despite his academic success. Sleep eluded him, and his once electric enthusiasm for learning dimmed, replaced by constant fatigue and disinterest.

Every thought, decision, and action taken from a place of alignment contributes to a more harmonious, effective, and fulfilling life.

One pivotal day, Alex had a breakdown. After pulling yet another all-nighter, he found himself sitting in the campus library, staring blankly at his computer screen. No matter how he tried to focus, his mind was a foggy mess. For the first time in his life, Alex couldn't think his way out of his predicament.

After a few weeks in our meditation course, Alex began to realize he was ignoring his physical, emotional, and spiritual needs. Initially resistant, he decided to make some changes. He began incorporating regular exercise into his routine, not just for physical health, but to clear his mind and release stress. He allowed himself to feel and acknowledge his emotions, realizing that they, too, had valuable lessons to offer. Meditation and mindfulness practices became part of his daily life, guiding him to connect with a deeper sense of self and purpose.

As Alex started to nourish all aspects of his being—physical, mental, emotional, and spiritual—he felt a newfound balance and fulfillment. Yes, his academic performance improved, which was great, but what truly surprised him was the joy and enthusiasm for life he rediscovered after so many years. Reflecting on his journey, Alex realized he'd been convinced that living solely in his mind was the right approach, believing the other parts of himself were unnecessary distractions. But embracing a wholistic approach showed him the harmony and richness in life that his intellect alone could never provide. He found that when all parts of him worked together, he experienced a depth and satisfaction beyond anything he'd known before.

Let's Practice . . .

It's very common to pay closer attention to one or two aspects of yourself, often influenced by society, your upbringing, and even what you're naturally good at. In other words, you probably have a body or two—like your mental or physical body—that gets most of your attention, while others—like your emotional or spiritual sides—get ignored or pushed aside. Let's shed some light on this and figure out which aspects of yourself you're most attuned to, and which ones might need a bit more love and care.

Take a deep 5-Phase Breath and go inside for a moment. Get honest and real with yourself and rank your bodies (physical, mental, emotional, and spiritual) in order of the greatest connection—or most comfortable to least comfortable. There is no right or wrong here; you are simply building awareness. For example, if you are the most comfortable in your physical body, this would be ranked #1. If you are the least comfortable in your mental body, this would be ranked #4. Now explain why you ranked them in this order and explore how this shows up in your life.

Here is an example from Tahnya, a sophomore in Kinesiology:

I ranked physical as #1, emotional as #2, spiritual as #3, and mental as #4. I said this because I am very physically oriented. I feel my physical body is my best friend. I am very active, and I enjoy feeling physical sensations—hunger, thirst, fatigue, energy. I ranked my mental body as #4 because I think that thinking is overrated. It tends to steer me wrong, especially when I get caught up in my ego, which causes me to compare myself with others.

Journal Prompts . . .

1. How does the awareness of the four bodies shift or change my perspective about how I create health and alignment in my life?
2. Which bodies could use more of my attention? The reason I think this is . . .
3. Something I can do about this is . . .

Bringing It All Together

Recognizing that the full human experience comes from engaging with *all* of you, empowers you to move, think, feel, and connect in transformative ways. Think of the story of the blind men and the elephant—the elephant isn't just a trunk, an ear, or a side; it's a complete entity, just like you. You are a physical, mental, emotional, and spiritual being. When you nurture your thoughts, emotions, physical sensations, and spirit, you'll notice how each one uniquely contributes to your overall well-being. It's this synergy, where each part supports and enhances the others, that brings true depth and richness to your life. By embracing a wholistic approach, you'll experience how all the different parts of your life connect, helping you feel more balanced and fulfilled.

CONGRATULATIONS
ON COMPLETING
PART ONE!

Oh, the places you'll go!

—DR. SEUSS

Throughout Part One, you've been laying down the essential groundwork for your mindfulness journey. Just like any adventure, having a sturdy foundation makes everything smoother and more rewarding. You've delved into the art of mindful breathing, embraced the beginner's mind, anchored yourself in the precious present, and embarked on the transformative path of living wholistically. You've successfully gathered all the crucial elements needed for the journey ahead. This is a perfect moment to take a step back and celebrate your progress.

Breathe in, breathe out.

Even if you decide not to venture further on this journey, recognize that you've already accomplished a great deal. These foundational principles are empowering, insightful, and brimming with sustainable wisdom. Remember, it's not about perfection; it's about the practice. Every moment you deliberately live upon these foundations, you are living mindfully.

Now, with the foundations in place, get ready to elevate your mindfulness journey.

A journey of a thousand miles begins with a single step.

—LAO TZU

Remember, it's not about perfection; it's about the practice.

Imagine, you decide to embark on a grand expedition, such as climbing a mountain that has captivated you from afar. From a distance, the mountain appears insurmountable—its peak shrouded in clouds with no discernible path in sight, making you wonder if you can truly find your way. As you get closer, you see a trailhead with signposts that reassure you, "Yes, you are heading the right way." Once you set foot on the path, an overwhelming sense of guidance, support, and direction envelops you. The trail and the surrounding foliage act like steadfast guardrails, ensuring you stay on course. With each step you take, what once seemed daunting unfolds into a series of manageable actions. By simply staying on the path—putting one foot in front of the other— you find yourself steadily ascending.

In life, much like climbing a mountain, establishing a consistent practice is like discovering a trailhead—it provides direction and draws you toward your ultimate destination. These simple daily practices serve as your paths to consistent progress on your journey. *The practice becomes the path!* And while there are countless practices and paths to explore, we will delve into some of the most traveled routes to achieving a life of Zen. These practices will guide you toward your own summit of inner peace and fulfillment, one step at a time.

You'll begin by unlocking the power of intentionality, guiding you toward a life aligned with your deepest values. Next, you'll uncover the art of meditation, finding your unique path to truth and peace. You'll then experience the transformative practice of guided visualization and tap in to the profound benefits of gratitude, setting the stage for a journey filled with joy and success. Finally, by following your natural path to Zen, you'll ground yourself and reconnect with the natural world around you. Each chapter provides a stepping stone to deeper mindfulness, offering new insights and practices to elevate your journey.

Let's embark on this next adventure together—there's so much more to discover!

PART 2

EMBODYING THE
PRACTICES

SIX

BECOMING INTENTIONAL

YOUR PATH TO LIVING A LIFE BY DESIGN

The secret to change is to focus all of your energy not on fighting the old, but on building the new.

—SOCRATES

I n Part One, you established the foundations and gathered essential tools for your mindfulness journey. You learned about the importance of paying attention to your breath and embracing a beginner's mind. You experienced the value of living in the precious present and attending to all aspects of your being—physical, mental, emotional, and spiritual. These foundational principles are not just stepping stones—they are your steadfast allies, ready to support you throughout every twist and turn of your journey. When you choose to employ them in your daily routine, they will become an integral part of your everyday living experience, providing clarity and energy.

With your foundations in place, it's now time to venture out into your next quest. Beginning with the power of your intention, you will explore, practice, and integrate a variety of mindfulness exercises into your daily routine, while the foundations you've built will continually support and empower you.

A Meaningful Journey Begins with Intention

The start of every journey is impacted by the energy and focus you put into your intention. Intention is ignored or belittled by the "unconscious traveler," who scurries about in a rush to get to where they are going, without regard to how they want to experience their next adventure. But for the conscious, mindful traveler, such as yourself, the intention of the journey is at the forefront of their awareness—they understand that intention-setting sets the tone for all decisions, actions, and behaviors.

Intention is the precursor to your outcome.
Intend wisely.

—GARY ZUKAV

Once, in a small village nestled in the foothills of the Himalayas, there lived a wise and revered sage. His wisdom and serenity were known far and wide, and pilgrims often traveled great distances to seek his guidance. One day, two pilgrims arrived at the sage's hermitage. They had both walked for days, each seeking enlightenment and a deeper understanding of life. The sage welcomed them with kind eyes and a gentle smile.

The first pilgrim was eager and restless. He spoke quickly, "O Wise One, I have come seeking enlightenment. I have studied many texts and practiced various disciplines, but still, I do not find peace. What must I do?" The sage replied, "To find peace, you must go to the river at dawn each day, fill this vessel with water, and meditate upon the sunrise. Let this be your practice for the next thirty days." The first pilgrim, though skeptical, accepted the sage's direction and set off with the vessel.

The second pilgrim approached more composed. She bowed respectfully and said, "O Sage, I have come in search of inner peace and purpose. I wish to live a life of meaning and joy." The sage gazed at her intently and replied, "You, too, shall go to the river at dawn each day. But as you fill this vessel with water, I want you to set a clear intention for your day, one that aligns with your values, aspirations, and the way you want to feel. Do this for the next thirty days." The second pilgrim nodded thoughtfully and took the vessel, feeling a deep sense of purpose.

Thirty days passed, and the two pilgrims returned to the hermitage. The first pilgrim looked weary and disheartened. He had performed the task but found no solace. "O Sage, I did as you asked, yet I am unchanged. The practice seemed meaningless to me," he lamented. The sage turned to the second pilgrim. She was radiant and calm. "O Wise One," she began, "each morning, as I filled the vessel, I set a clear intention for how I wanted to feel throughout my day. I sought to feel kindness, gratitude, and peace. It transformed my views, my beliefs, and my interactions with all that was around me—the animals, the plants, and the humans. I feel a profound connection to my purpose and a sense of inner peace." The sage smiled knowingly and said, "The essence of your practice lies in the intention you set. Without intention, actions can feel empty and unfulfilling. *But with a clear and heartfelt intention, even the simplest tasks become infused with meaning and can transform your life.*"

This parable illustrates that the power of creating intention can turn ordinary activities into profound practices that nurture the soul and guide you toward inner peace and fulfillment. By aligning daily actions with clear intentions, you bring purpose and joy into your life, creating a deeper sense of connection with your values and aspirations.

Mindful intention-setting emphasizes how you want to feel rather than what you aim to achieve. By identifying how you wish to feel throughout your day, or in the next hour, or in each moment, you create meaningful markers and boundaries that guide your decisions and actions, ensuring they remain on track and in alignment with your desired emotional state.

Unlike goal-setting, which zeroes in on specific outcomes, mindful intention-setting emphasizes the journey—the multitude of moments and emotions that guide you toward your aspirations. This is where your true power lies: *in shaping your own experience*. You can't control every outcome, but you can control how you feel and respond along the way.

For example, aiming for an A in a class might seem like a solid goal. But when you shift to intention-setting, you focus instead on how you want to feel throughout the process. (See the difference?) Consider this: If your goal is to get an "A" and you end up with an A- or B+, it's easy to feel like you've failed, which can be discouraging. However, if your intention is to learn and feel inspired, joyful, confident, and dedicated throughout your studies, you're concentrating on aspects you can control. You can't dictate how your professor grades or how you stack up against your classmates. But if you achieve an A- or B+ while experiencing the feelings you intended, you can genuinely feel proud of your commitment and growth. This approach places your focus on the journey rather than the destination, allowing you to derive fulfillment and pride from your efforts regardless of external outcomes.

> Mindful intention-setting emphasizes how you want to feel rather than what you aim to achieve.

You are always creating your life.
You either create it by design or live it by default.

—MARY MORRISEY

Living *Without* vs. *With* Intention

Let's take a look at two very different scenarios. In the first scenario, Tyler (remember him from the beginning of the book?) rushes through his day with no intention at all. In the second scenario, Emily capitalizes on setting a mindful intention to direct her day in a way that feels good for her.

Tyler woke to his blaring 8:00 a.m. alarm. He groggily reached out to silence it, realizing he had hit snooze one too many times. Hurriedly, he threw on clothes, grabbed a piece of cold pizza, and rushed out the door. On the way to his first class, Tyler felt a rising wave of anxiety. His hurried steps carried him past friends and sunshine that he barely noticed. Entering the lecture hall breathless, he slid into a seat just as the professor began. Throughout the class, Tyler felt sleepy and scattered, his notes disorganized, his mind wandering from topic to topic.

After the lecture, he drifted to the library and tried to study, but he found it impossible to focus. The pages of his textbooks blurred together, and his mind kept jumping from last night's poor sleep to tomorrow's paper deadline. His interactions with friends felt hollow; their laughter didn't reach him. By noon, Tyler realized he had forgotten to pack a lunch. He grabbed a soggy sandwich from a campus café and ate alone, feeling disconnected and out of sync with himself and others. The afternoon classes dragged on, each minute feeling both too slow and too fast. By 3:00 p.m., Tyler's energy was spent, and his thoughts were a chaotic mess.

Returning home that evening, Tyler collapsed onto his bed, mindlessly scrolling through social media. A hollow emptiness echoed inside him, a sense that his day had vanished without him creating any meaningful impact. Gazing up at the ceiling, he felt an urgent need for something different, though he was uncertain what that might be or how to attain it. This feeling of disconnection seemed almost normal, as he observed his friends drifting through the same aimless routine.

Emily had set her alarm an hour early. She had learned about the power of intention-setting through her mindfulness course the semester before. At 7:00 a.m., she woke to the light sound of crickets chirping. Sitting up, she took a deep breath, looked out the window, took a moment to stretch, then went to the kitchen for a warm cup of lemon water before sitting down to her journal. During her morning writing, she discovered that her intention for the day was to feel grounded and focused. She wrote it in her journal and repeated it to herself as an affirmation (a positive statement about yourself, as if it is occurring in the moment): "I feel grounded and focused." This would guide her day.

Walking to her first class, Emily noticed the morning air, the warmth of the sun on her face and the sound of her footsteps as she neared the building. During the lecture, she took organized notes and stayed engaged, reminding herself to think the thoughts and do the actions required to stay grounded and focused. She met her friend Mia under a tree for lunch. During their conversation, Mia invited her to an impromptu shopping trip at a nearby mall. Remembering her intention, Emily politely declined, saying, "I have some studying I want to stay focused on today." She knew the shopping trip would be really fun, but it would scatter her energy and veer her away from her intention of feeling grounded and focused.

In the library for her study session, she set a mini-intention: "I want to feel accomplished by the time I leave the library." When a classmate suggested they chat instead, she gently said, "I need to concentrate right now, but let's catch up later." Her focused study time left her feeling like a rock star. When entering a club meeting that evening, Emily felt not only grounded and focused from her morning intention, but also proud and excited about the actions she had taken during the day to stay in alignment. It had been a really full day, but she felt energized. She had allowed her intention to steer her decisions and actions, and this synergy instilled in her a sense of confidence and ease as she connected with her fellow club members. When discussions drifted off-topic, she adeptly guided them back, subtly reminding everyone of the meeting's objectives. Her intention enabled her to uphold both a sense of grounding and focus all day long. As she returned to her dorm, Emily reflected on a deeply fulfilling day, grateful for the direction her intention had provided. She was particularly appreciative of how well she had been able to steer herself back on track whenever distractions arose.

Notice the stark contrast between Tyler and Emily's experiences. Tyler resembled a puppet on a string, reacting to the whims of his alarm, a hectic schedule, mounting anxiety, poor nutritional choices, an inability to focus, low energy, and thoughts that normalized his restless experience. In sharp contrast, Emily took on the role of creator of her day. She proactively identified how she wanted to feel, chose thoughts and actions that were in alignment with her intention, and embraced elevated emotions of appreciation and gratitude.

Now that you have a grasp on the power of intention-setting, let's work together to find the perfect intention for the rest of your mindful journey. With these simple steps, you'll create a powerful and meaningful intention that will guide and enrich your path ahead.

Creating a Mindful Intention

1. Preparation: Settle into a serene, distraction-free space. Allow yourself to sit quietly for 5-10 minutes, giving yourself full permission to simply be.

* Engage with your breath by completing three 5-Phase Breath cycles (see chapter 2).
* Invoke a sense of curiosity by adopting a beginner's mind (refer to chapter 3).
* Gently tap into your emotional body (see chapter 5), gradually opening to the full spectrum of your emotions.

- When this feels complete, gently bring your attention back to the space around you and thoughtfully answer the following questions in your journal:
- How do I want to feel while traveling on this mindful journey? How do I want to feel by the end of the journey? Reflect on the feelings currently absent from your life and consider those you wish to invite in and experience more fully.
- What values or principles are most important to me in my daily life? Identify key values, such as peace, focus, compassion, resilience, connection, or balance.

2. Once you have your responses, close your eyes and visualize your ideal outcome. Picture yourself living out this intention. Imagine the positive changes and how you use your chosen intention to handle derailments. Notice how it feels to live in alignment. Journal your responses so you have them captured on paper.

3. Allow yourself to luxuriate in this sensation a little longer. Let yourself fully experience the benefits of your intention. Envision the sensation of having a guiding force that positively influences your thoughts, decisions, and actions. Reflect on who else would benefit from this transformation. Consider how you would navigate through life differently with this influence. Compile a list of all the benefits you would reap from embarking on an intentional mindfulness journey.

4. Now that you have identified your intention from a place of insight and alignment, write it in your journal in a succinct and simple format. Use these examples from other college students to get started:

- "My intention for my mindfulness journey is to feel peace and ease."
- "My intention for my mindfulness journey is to feel confident and focused."
- "My intention for my mindfulness journey is to feel open and curious."

- "My intention for my mindfulness journey is to feel joy and lightness."

You've just accomplished an empowering and insightful step toward realizing your journey's full potential. Now, let's delve deeper into the specific benefits of living out this intention. When your creative mind recognizes the rewards associated with your efforts and actions, it is more inclined to engage enthusiastically, releasing any resistance and fostering forward momentum.

5. Create a list of benefits. What specific benefits will you experience when you approach and live your mindfulness journey with intention? For example, if your intention is to feel peace and ease, the benefits might be:

- " I will experience less drama in my relationships."
- " I will sleep better and not feel cranky during the day."
- " I will enjoy school."

Now that you have identified your intention *and* the benefits associated with it, let's clarify which actions you are willing to take to achieve your intention—because without action, your intention remains powerless.

Intention without action is merely a fantasy.
Action without intention is simply chaos.

—PETER MCWILLIAMS

6. Write down at least three actions you are willing to take.
Play with these, getting as specific as possible. Here are a few examples:

- "I will schedule time for mindfulness practices at least three days per week for at least 20-30 minutes per day."

- "I will complete the suggested readings and the exercises in each chapter."

- "I am committed to dedicating at least one hour per week to learning and practicing mindfulness."

Consider what might get in the way of implementing the actions that will move you toward what you truly want. This could include limited thinking, a full schedule, lack of motivation/drive, etc. Also, consider what you might be willing to sacrifice to act in alignment with your intention. Will you have the time, energy, and resources to commit to these actions? Make plans now concerning how you will overcome obstacles as they present themselves.

Now combine your intention statement with the actions you will take. Craft your intention in a way that is meaningful and compelling for you. Imagine it as a powerful magnet, pulling you toward it, fueling your passion and excitement to achieve your goals.

Here are two examples to help you get started:

- "My intention for this journey is to feel peace and ease, which will help me experience less drama in my relationships. What I will do to achieve this is dedicate at least one hour per week to learning and practicing mindfulness techniques while also saying no to actions that increase anxiety."

- "My intention for this journey is to feel confident and focused, which will improve my sleep patterns so I'm not so cranky during the day. What I will do to achieve this is to practice mindfulness exercises at least four times per week, especially the ones before bedtime."

In review, intention-setting is a powerful practice that starts with identifying the primary feeling or state of being you want to cultivate in your life—whether it's peace, joy, confidence, or something else. Next, consider the benefits associated with this desired state. For example, if you aim to feel more confident, the benefits might include improved relationships, better performance at work or school, and a greater sense of personal satisfaction. Finally, outline the actions you are willing to take to achieve this state. These actions might include daily affirmations, setting clear goals, or practicing self-care routines. By integrating these steps—defining the desired feeling, understanding its benefits, and committing to specific actions—you create a clear, actionable roadmap to manifesting your intention into reality.

Ready to create your ultimate intention for your mindfulness journey? Let's put it all together:

My intention is _____ .

The benefits are _____ .

The actions I will take are _____ .

Use your answers to refine your intention statement and write the final version in the box below.

Living Life by Design

By slowing down, breathing deeply, and crafting your intention from a place of personal alignment, you harness your inner power and step into the role of the creator of your experience. Clarifying your intention and outlining the actionable steps you are willing to take transforms you into the architect of your life, deliberately and purposefully designing your journey with intention. Mary Morrisey, a best-selling author and personal development coach, summarizes the power of an intention-setting lifestyle as follows:

You have the power to design your life.

> You are always creating your life. You either create it by design or you live the life you get by default. When you live by default, you're reacting to circumstances, rather than taking control and creating the life you desire. You move through your days being tossed to and fro by what happens outside of you, with no clear direction, purpose, or intention. This often leads to a sense of dissatisfaction, because deep down, your soul knows you are meant for more.
>
> Living by design, on the other hand, means taking deliberate and intentional steps towards your dreams. It means defining what you truly want, setting clear goals, and taking inspired action towards them every day. It's about aligning your thoughts, words, and actions with your highest vision. By doing so, you step into your power as a creator of your own reality, and experience the profound joy and fulfillment that comes from living a life that is fully aligned with your purpose and passions.

Stated simply, you have the power to design your life. You can choose to live with intention and create experiences that light you up and bring you joy, or you can play victim to life and fool yourself into thinking you have no control of your life path.

As a college student, you might scoff at the notion that you can craft your life by design rather than by default. It may feel as if you have a myriad of puppeteers pulling your strings—ranging from professors and guidance counselors to parents and friends. Sometimes it can feel even bigger, as though the very institution of college or the government itself holds sway over your life. But when you truly grasp the power of intentional living and embrace its transformative potential, you ascend from being a passive puppet on a string to becoming the empowered architect of your life. Remember, you are not merely a passenger on this voyage, you are the captain of your destiny. So, stride forward with unwavering confidence and insatiable curiosity, knowing that each step you take is a deliberate creation.

Now that we've explored the basics of intention-setting, let's delve into some additional practices that can help you focus your energy on building new experiences with intentionality. These methods, from "segment intending" to the "doorway practice" to simple self-reflection, can further support and enhance your intentions, making them an integral part of your daily life.

Segment intending is a powerful technique to help you bring clarity and purpose to different parts of your day. The idea is to mentally divide your day into distinct segments, such as attending lectures, studying, socializing with friends, or participating in extracurricular activities. Before each segment begins, take a moment to pause and set a specific intention for that period. For instance, before heading to a lecture, you might set an intention to feel the joy of accomplishment, identifying the action to be attentive. When meeting friends for lunch, your aim might be to feel the joy of connection, identifying your action to be fully present. By consciously setting these intentions, you align your thoughts and actions with your desired feelings, bringing more mindfulness and control into your daily experiences. This practice not only helps in reducing stress and increasing productivity, but it also ensures that each moment of your day is approached with intention and purpose.

The doorway practice, a tradition rooted in Buddhist mindfulness, is a simple yet profound method for cultivating intentional living. Every time you pass through a doorway, whether it's entering your apartment, walking into the dining hall, or stepping into the gym, you use this transition as a moment to reset with a fresh intention. For example, before walking into a dining hall, you might pause at the doorway to set an intention to eat your meal mindfully and with gratitude. Prior to entering a study group session, you might affirm an intention to be collaborative and focused. This practice transforms ordinary moments into opportunities for mindfulness, helping you to carry your intentions more consistently throughout the day. By anchoring intentions to your passing through doorways, you weave mindfulness into the fabric of your daily life, promoting a more intentional, conscious way of being.

Self-reflection is a powerful tool for building and sustaining your intentions. By regularly pausing to check in with yourself, you gain insight into your progress and where adjustments can be made. Think of it like driving down the center of a lane: If you veer too far to the right, you risk ending up in the ditch; too far to the left, and you cross the line into oncoming traffic. Just as a skilled driver makes continuous, subtle adjustments to stay on course, self-reflection allows you to evaluate your actions and intentions, ensuring you stay aligned with your goals. This practice allows you to acknowledge your achievements, identify areas where you might be drifting off course, and make necessary changes before any major issues arise. By integrating regular self-reflection into your intention-setting process, you empower yourself to stay on track and navigate life with greater mindfulness and control.

Finding an image that captures the feeling you want to embody can also be incredibly powerful. The brain processes visual information much more effectively than words, making images a potent tool for reinforcing your intentions. When you choose an image that resonates with the feeling or state you aspire to experience—such as a peaceful beach for calmness, an inspiring leader for confidence, or a joyful gathering for connection—your brain recognizes and internalizes these visuals more deeply. This visual cue helps your brain to activate and align its resources to manifest that desired state into reality. The repeated exposure to this image acts as a constant reminder and motivator, subconsciously directing your actions and decisions toward achieving your intention. By integrating images into your intention-setting practice, you harness the brain's natural ability to translate visual stimuli into concrete actions, making your goals more tangible and achievable.

Attaching an image to a long-term intention is especially valuable as life's demands can easily steer you off course. Visual reminders have a unique way of anchoring your focus, making it easier to stay aligned with your goals. When you place the image where you see it often—whether on your home screen, by your laptop, on your bathroom mirror, or in your backpack—it serves as a constant nudge to both your conscious and unconscious mind. This frequent exposure reinforces the intention, acting as a compass that consistently guides you back on track, no matter how hectic life becomes. By integrating these visual cues into your daily environment, you create a steady reminder of your aspirations, helping you maintain clarity and commitment toward reaching your long-term goals.

Let's Practice . . .

You created an intention for the rest of your mindfulness journey; now create an intention, using the same steps, for something else you want in your life—big or small.

Find an image that depicts the *feeling* you want to have in connection with this intention. Place it where you will see it every day.

Self-reflect, at least once per week, on how your thoughts and actions are staying in alignment with your intention. Journal about this and then ask the question, "Are my actions in alignment with my intention?"

Celebrate your aligned actions and/or shift your actions to realign.

Journal Prompts . . .

1. What comes to mind when I think about creating my life out of default or by design is . . .
2. Something I really want to create in my life is . . .
3. Imagine that you have already achieved one of your intentions (big or small). Describe how this feels. Identify the actions you will take to achieve this feeling. Use vivid detail to paint a picture of this ideal scenario.

Bringing It All Together

Intention-setting is an adaptable practice that can be applied to virtually any aspect of your life, whether it's focused on a study session in the library or landing your ideal job after graduation. By consciously setting an intention, you are identifying how you want to feel—this becomes the driving factor. Then you can clarify the actions that will steer you toward that feeling. This practice transforms everyday moments into opportunities for mindful living and empowers you to approach both minor details and major milestones with the same level of intention and mindfulness. Remember, you are always creating! You don't have a choice in life *but* to create. The power lies in understanding that you are either creating by design or creating by default. You get to choose.

Now that you have gotten the hang of setting intentions, let's dive into something that can supercharge them: *meditation*. This powerful practice helps you stay focused, calm, and clear-minded, making it easier to stick to your goals. Ready to explore how meditation can boost your intentional living? Dive into the next chapter when you're ready.

SEVEN

MEDITATING YOUR WAY TO ZEN

YOUR PATH TO TRUTH AND PEACE

Meditation is not a way of making your mind quiet. It is a way of entering into the quiet that is already there—buried under the 50,000 thoughts the average person thinks every day.

—DEEPAK CHOPRA

Once upon a time, the gods convened to discuss where they should hide the ultimate truth, so humans would have to earn the right to discover it. One god suggested hiding it at the top of the highest mountain. Another proposed the

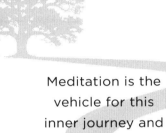

Meditation is the vehicle for this inner journey and the secret sauce that enriches every external venture.

deepest ocean; yet another recommended placing it on the far side of the moon. But Brahma, the wisest of them all, shook his head and said, "No, we will hide the truth inside humans themselves. They will search high and low, scaling mountains and exploring oceans, traveling to the far corners of the earth and beyond. Yet all the while, the truth they seek will be nestled deep within their own hearts and minds. Only those who truly look inward and embark on the inner journey will discover it, and in doing so, they will find not just the truth, but their true Self." And so, the gods hid the truth within each human, ensuring the journey to enlightenment would also be a journey of self-discovery.

This parable beautifully underscores the theme that the most profound truths and answers lie within our Selves, waiting to be discovered through introspection and self-awareness. But how does one embark on the journey inward to uncover their inner truths? How do you delve within yourself to find the answers, especially when it seems so much easier to seek answers from those who've already done the inner work?

The solution lies in slowing down, pausing, and taking a deep breath. Allow yourself the grace to step out of the relentless current of chaos, excess, and overwhelm—despite society's insistence that you must perpetually remain in motion. Remind yourself that within you already resides a vast wellspring of wisdom, intuition, and truth. The only obstacle is your reluctance to connect with your own internal reservoir of guidance.

Creating your life by design, as we discussed in the last chapter, can often be misconstrued as an "external" endeavor, focused on outer circumstances, adventures, and experiences. However, as you will discover in this chapter, the most profound transformation lies along the journey inward—a pathway to true calm, centeredness, and alignment with your Self (capitalized to signify your authentic Self beyond the confines of the ego). Meditation is the vehicle for this inner journey and the secret sauce that enriches every external venture, grounding your existence in a wellspring of inner peace, clarity, and a Zen state of mind and body.

The Transformative Benefits of Meditation

The benefits of meditation are limitless. Meditation is a transformative practice that serves as a gateway to your inner Self. Many students who have embraced meditation report a plethora of benefits, including:

- Developing greater self-trust
- Silencing the incessant chatter of the inner critic
- Enhancing relationships with Self and others
- Managing busy schedules with increased ease
- Excelling in both academic and athletic pursuits
- Boosting creativity
- Reducing perceived stress levels
- Making informed choices regarding activities, classes, friends, and career opportunities
- Heightening self-awareness
- Bolstering confidence
- Improving overall physical health
- Increasing motivation

Wow! After reading this extensive, though not exhaustive, list of benefits, I can't help but think, "I want that for myself!"

How about you?

Which benefits resonate most strongly with you?

Take a moment to highlight those that catch your attention and hold particular importance for you. Then, record them in your journal. As we discussed in the previous chapter, clearly identifying what you want and need sets your mind in motion, working toward achieving your truest desires. Meditation is one of the most powerful tools at your disposal to claim these benefits—and its practice is free of charge, has no negative side effects, and can be done anywhere, anytime.

Let's drop into a deeper understanding of what meditation is—and what it is not. Historically, from the 5th century BCE, meditation has been a core practice of the Buddhist tradition. The Buddhist concept of meditation, or *bhāvanā* (meaning "mental development" or "cultivation"), is defined as a systematic practice designed to cultivate clarity, concentration, and insight. In essence, it serves as a gateway to your inner Self. Its three core principles are **1. Ethical Conduct** (treating self and others with love and respect); **2. Mental Discipline** (improving concentration and mental development); and **3. Wisdom** (gaining insights leading to an understanding of the nature of reality and fostering enlightenment). In essence, Buddhist meditation is a comprehensive practice that aims to develop mental calmness, concentration, and insight, which together pave the way for spiritual awakening and liberation from the cycle of suffering.

Beyond its Buddhist roots, meditation encompasses a wide array of practices and philosophies that transcend any single tradition. Many individuals engage in various styles of meditation that span diverse cultural contexts and personal preferences, including *Transcendental Meditation* (TM), *Guided Meditation*, *Yoga Nidra* (Yogic Sleep), *Moving Meditation*, *Nature Meditation*, *Contemplative Prayer*, *Mindfulness-Based Stress Reduction* (MBSR), *Loving-Kindness Meditation* (Metta), *Visualization Meditation*, and *Shamanic Journeying*, just to name a few.

Now let's take a moment to explore what meditation is *not*, which can help dispel any common misconceptions about the practice.

First of all, **meditation is not just relaxation.** While relaxation can be a byproduct of meditation, the practice itself aims for deeper mental clarity, awareness, and insight. It's about conscious engagement with one's inner world rather than mere stress relief.

Also, despite widespread misunderstanding, **meditation is not escapism.** It is not a way to avoid problems or escape reality. Instead, meditation encourages confronting and understanding your thoughts and emotions mindfully.

Meditation is not about emptying the mind. Contrary to popular belief, it does not require achieving a completely blank slate. Rather, meditation is about observing your thoughts without attachment and gently bringing your focus back to the present moment. This misconception can be particularly limiting, as many people believe they must attain a state of *tabula rasa*—the Latin term for "blank slate"—to be successful meditators. While you may indeed experience moments, or even micro-moments, of mental stillness, much of your energy during meditation is directed toward cultivating awareness and bringing your thoughts back to the present moment.

Although meditation has roots in various religious traditions, **meditation is not inherently a religious practice.** Many meditate purely for psychological, physical, or emotional benefits without any religious connotation.

Meditation is not instantaneous. The benefits of meditation often emerge gradually and require consistent practice. It is not a quick fix, but rather a journey that unfolds over time with patience and perseverance. Many find that its rewards are not immediate, necessitating the cultivation of patience—a virtue that is itself among the many benefits of meditation.

Additionally, **meditation is not a performance**. There is no "right" or "wrong" way to meditate, nor does it require attaining a specific state or outcome. It is a deeply personal practice that varies from individual to individual, allowing each person to find their unique path to inner peace and clarity.

I often have students comment that they cannot sit still for meditation. If that's you, there's good news! **Meditation is not only a seated practice.** While many forms of meditation involve sitting, it's not limited to this posture. Walking meditation, mindful eating, and other activities can also be forms of meditation. Even washing the dishes or taking a shower can be practiced meditatively.

Meditation is not exclusive to any one group. It's accessible to everyone, regardless of age, background, or belief system. There's no need for special skills, attire, or equipment to begin meditating.

Although it may appear passive, meditation requires active engagement with your mind and often involves a deliberate effort to cultivate mindfulness, compassion, or concentration. It is crucial to understand that **meditation is not a passive activity,** nor is it solely about positive thinking. **Meditation is not about forcing a positive mindset or suppressing negative thoughts.** Instead, meditation embraces the acceptance of all thoughts and emotions without judgment, fostering a balanced and insightful perspective.

By outlining what meditation is not, we are better able to understand its true nature and dispel common misconceptions, allowing for a more accurate and meaningful engagement with the practice.

A Case in Point

Remember Tyler? His meditation journey didn't go smoothly at first. When he started to practice, Tyler chose to meditate lying down. The quiet environment and focus on relaxation quickly lulled him to sleep, and more than once, he found himself snoring in the middle of a class meditation session, drawing amused glances and light giggles from his fellow students. It was clear that lying down wasn't the best approach for Tyler to stay awake and attentive.

Because he really wanted to experience the benefits that meditation offered and was determined to make progress, Tyler chose to stay in the game and try something different. He moved from lying down to staying seated, hoping this would help keep him from slipping into slumberland. This worked; it helped him stay awake, but now he noticed his mind racing and jumping from one thought to another (often referred to as "Monkey Mind"). He found himself thinking about upcoming assignments, social plans, and worries about the future. It was frustrating, but Tyler refused to give up. Instead, whenever his mind wandered, he practiced gently bringing his focus back to his breath. Gradually, the racing thoughts began to slow down. Tyler was no longer overwhelmed by a torrent of thoughts; he was arriving at a newfound clarity about his thoughts and feelings. He realized that meditation wasn't about having a completely blank mind, but about observing his thoughts without getting entangled in them.

As weeks turned into months, Tyler's practice deepened, allowing him to quiet his mind enough to experience profound moments of stillness and peace. He discovered an expanding awareness of his inner Self, aligning with what he had been taught in class—that meditation serves as a gateway to one's true nature. This inward journey brought him back to his center, realigning him with a deeper sense of grounding, connection, and self-awareness. As a result, he became more attuned to his thoughts and emotions, allowing him to manage his stress with greater ease and make decisions with a clearer sense of inner knowing and self-trust.

Tyler's improved focus spilled over into his academic life, and he found it easier to concentrate during study sessions and exams. His relationships with friends and family also benefited, as he became more present and empathetic in conversations. Tyler's practice of meditation, like all new ventures, progressed from initial effort and frustration to a place of comfort and ease, ultimately becoming a cornerstone of his daily routine and interactions. It provided him with a sanctuary of calm amidst the busyness of college life.

Tyler's journey is an empowering example of the ups and downs that come with starting something new, including a meditation practice. More importantly, it highlights how sticking with it and learning about yourself can lead to incredible benefits. As Tyler kept at it, the little insights he gained snowballed into major momentum. Each breakthrough in understanding himself fueled his progress even more, helping him handle stress better, make clearer decisions, and stay grounded no matter what college life threw his way. It became his positive feedback loop that kept getting better the more he dropped into his meditation practice.

Creating Your Space: How to Create External and Internal Space for Meditation

Let's face it—college life can be chaotic, and finding a moment to meditate can sometimes feel impossible. But imagine having a little sanctuary where you can escape, even if just for a few minutes. That's what creating space for meditation is all about. It's not just about making a comfy spot to sit; it's about creating a vibe that helps you chill out and tune in. We're talking about crafting both your external space—like your room or a cozy corner—and your internal space—your mindset. Rest assured, with just a few simple steps, you can turn any spot into a peaceful retreat that helps you unwind and recharge.

Creating Your External Space

1. Choose a Distraction-Free Location: Pick a spot where you can feel comfortable and safe, free from disruptions. This will enable your nervous system to settle down, allowing you to close your eyes and fully relax without worry.

2. Clear the Clutter: Opt for an area that is clean and organized. Even with your eyes closed, your mind can sense disorder and chaos around you, which might inhibit your ability to truly unwind.

3. Avoid Meditating in Bed: While your bedroom can be an ideal spot for meditation, lying on your bed could be counterproductive. For your entire life, you've trained your body to associate your bed with sleep. Therefore, if you lie down, you're likely to get sleepy. Instead, if you meditate in your bedroom, choose a seated position where your back is supported and you can sit upright, ensuring consistent airflow and alertness.

Creating Your Internal Space

1. Mind Dump: Before you dive into your meditation session, take a moment to unload everything that's weighing on your mind, body, emotions, and spirit. Grab a piece of paper and

jot down your thoughts and feelings—consider it a wholistic check-in. Open yourself up to what's happening
in each aspect of your life—physical, mental, emotional,
and spiritual. Approach this exercise as an observer, not
forming attachments or judgments to what you find,
just simply noticing.

2. Acceptance: Give yourself full permission to accept whatever comes to your awareness during this process. Remember,
all of it is valuable. Acceptance is key to creating an internal
space free from resistance and judgment, allowing you to enter a state of genuine mindfulness.

3. Create Your Intention: Now, connect with what you want
to feel during your meditation. Frame this as a clear intention: "My intention for this meditation is to feel _____
_____."

Even if you don't feel this way initially, simply setting the
intention creates room for the desired shift. For example,
"My intention for this meditation is to feel calm and relaxed." By articulating this intention, you set the stage for
your meditation to foster these feelings.

Let's Practice . . .

Today, we're diving into a step-by-step mindfulness
practice designed to help you find calm and presence
amid the chaos of college life. We'll start by clearing
mental clutter with a Mind Dump, then move into
a phase of Acceptance, and finally set a powerful Intention for our meditation. This structured approach
will guide you toward a more centered and peaceful
state. And for those who wish to deepen their practice, we'll conclude with an optional add-on called

Loving-Kindness Meditation—an incredible technique that fosters compassion and connection with yourself and others. Ready to get started? Let's create some inner harmony!

Step-by-Step Mindful Meditation Practice

1. **Find a Quiet Space:** Choose a calm, quiet place where you won't be disturbed. This could be a dedicated meditation spot or simply a quiet corner in your room.

2. **Mind Dump:** On a piece of paper, unload everything that's weighing on your mind, body, emotions, and spirit.

3. **Get Comfortable:** Sit in a comfortable position. You can sit on a chair with your feet flat on the ground, cross-legged on a meditation cushion, or in any position that feels good to you. Keep your back straight but relaxed, and rest your hands on your lap or knees.

4. **Close Your Eyes and Take a Few Deep Breaths:** Gently close your eyes and take three deep 5-Phase Breaths.

5. **Focus on Your Natural Breath:** Now let your breath return to its natural rhythm. Direct your attention to the sensation of breathing. Notice the cool air entering your nostrils and the warm air leaving. Feel the rise and fall of your chest or belly as you breathe in and out.

6. **Anchor Your Attention:** Choose one aspect of your breath to anchor your attention. It could be the sensation of the air passing through your nostrils, the movement of your chest, or the feeling of your abdomen rising and falling. Set your intention.

7. **Observe without Judgment:** Simply observe your breath without trying to change it. Notice its natural rhythm and how each inhalation and exhalation feels; be present with the experience of breathing.

8. **Notice When Your Mind Wanders:** It's natural for your mind to wander. You might start thinking about your to-do list, memories, or random thoughts. When

this happens, gently acknowledge that your mind has wandered without judgment.

9. **Gently Bring Your Attention Back to Your Breath:** When you notice your mind has wandered, gently and kindly bring your attention back to your breath. Use your chosen anchor (nostrils, chest, or abdomen) to refocus. It's important to be gentle with yourself—recognize that drifting thoughts are a normal part of meditation.

10. **Continue the Practice:** Continue this practice for the duration of your meditation session. Each time your mind wanders, calmly and repeatedly bring your focus back to your breath. Think of it as a process of training your attention.

11. **Set a Timer:** Begin with a manageable time, such as 5-10 minutes, and gradually increase it as you become more comfortable. Use a gentle timer to signal the end of your session without startling you, or choose a piece of music that plays for the duration of your ideal time frame.

Loving-Kindness Meditation Add-On

- **Generate Kindness for Yourself:** Silently repeat phrases such as, "May I be happy; may I be healthy; may I be safe; may I live with ease." Genuinely feel these good wishes.
- **Extend to a Loved One:** Think of someone you care about and mentally send them the same phrases: "May you be happy; may you be healthy; may you be safe; may you live with ease."
- **Expand to Others:** Include neutral persons and even those you have conflicts with, repeating the phrases for each: "May you be happy; may you be healthy; may you be safe; may you live with ease."

- **Embrace All Beings:** Finally, extend these wishes to all living beings, envisioning the world filled with love and kindness: "May all beings be happy; may all beings be healthy; may all beings be safe; may all beings live with ease."

12. **Gently Transition Out:** When your timer goes off, or your music ends, begin the cycle of three 5-Phase Breaths, bringing yourself back a little more with each breath. Slowly open your eyes, looking downward at first and gradually allowing your gaze to rise. Notice how you feel before moving out of your position.

13. **Reflect on Your Experience:** Take a moment to reflect on your meditation session. How did it feel to focus on your breath? Were you able to gently bring your attention back when it wandered? What was it like to practice the art of returning your focus without chastising or judging yourself? This self-reflection not only helps you glean valuable insights from your practice, but it also allows you to carry those insights into your daily life and future meditation sessions, thereby reinforcing the empowering benefits of your practice.

By incorporating simple meditation practices, such as sitting for a period paying attention to your breath, or engaging in a more focused practice like the Loving-Kindness Meditation, you'll feel more at peace and better equipped to handle academic, athletic, social, and work-related stress. These practices help you be kinder to yourself and others, building stronger connections and bringing more harmony into your life. Give them a try and watch how they make your journey calmer and kinder every day.

Journal Prompts . . .

1. **Reflect on Your Thoughts**. During my meditation session, the recurring thoughts or distractions that came up were . . . How I responded to these thoughts was . . .
2. **Observe Your Emotions.** The emotions that surfaced during my meditation were... How I can practice accepting these emotions without judgment in both meditation and daily life is . . .
3. **Evaluate Your Judgments.** A judgment or criticism I had about myself was . . . The specific thoughts or behaviors that triggered these judgments were . . . A way I can cultivate a more compassionate inner dialogue moving forward is . . .
4. **Notice the Impact on Daily Life.** How has my meditation practice affected my daily interactions, stress levels, and decision-making? Can I identify any positive changes or insights that have emerged from my consistent practice, and how have these influenced my overall well-being?

Bringing It All Together

The benefits of meditation for college students are profound and wide-ranging. By incorporating meditation into your daily routines, you can experience improved concentration, enhanced emotional health, increased self-awareness, and reduced stress levels. These advantages are empowering, providing a Zen state of mind and body that is essential for navigating the many demands of college life. Meditation provides a sanctuary of calm amidst the chaos, inviting you to connect with your true Self, where the proverbial gods have hidden your truths. This deep sense of grounding empowers you to make clearer decisions and take wise, deliberate actions that serve you and others for your highest good. Understanding that meditation is not about emptying the mind, but rather observing thoughts without attachment and gently bringing focus back to the present moment, you can embrace this practice as an active engagement with your inner world. Each small insight and breakthrough fuels further momentum, helping you manage stress more effectively and cultivate inner peace. Consistent practice and self-reflection, through tools such as journal prompts, allow you to integrate the lessons learned from meditation into every aspect of your life. In doing so, meditation becomes more than a practice—it transforms into a cornerstone of daily living, guiding you on a journey of continual growth, self-discovery, and empowerment.

Now that you have a solid foundation in understanding the practice of meditation, let's venture into the dynamic practice of visualization, which is a specialized style of meditation. Here, your imagination comes alive, transforming monochromatic thoughts into a vibrant kaleidoscope of technicolor possibilities—a place where anything is possible!

EIGHT

REDIRECTING THROUGH GUIDED VISUALIZATION

YOUR PATH TO CLARITY AND SUCCESS

Imagination is everything.
It is the preview of life's coming attractions.

—ALBERT EINSTEIN

A curious boy had become completely hooked on a simple compass his dad had given him. Despite its small size, the compass needle always seemed to point north, sparking endless questions in his mind about the invisible forces making it work. This early fascination set him on a path full of wonder and discovery.

As he got older, his curiosity grew stronger. By age 16, he started doing something that he called "thought experiments." He would visualize riding right alongside a beam of light, trying to figure out what it would look like if he could match its speed. It made him wonder things like, "What would a light wave look like if I was traveling next to it?"

These vivid mental images led him to some puzzling questions that the physics of his time just couldn't answer. But instead of giving up, he dug in deeper, and his relentless curiosity led to a massive breakthrough in understanding our universe.

That boy was none other than Albert Einstein. Yes, the same Einstein who rocked the world with his theory of special relativity in 1905. This theory changed how we think about space, time, and energy. He didn't just see formulas and equations; he saw pictures and felt gut-level intuitions. Einstein often described his creative process as one that didn't initially rely on words or numbers. Instead, he would form vibrant images in his mind and feel intuitive insights, which he would later translate into the mathematical equations and scientific papers that we revere today.

Later, Einstein turned those mental images into the groundbreaking science we now trust and rely upon. He once said, *"Imagination is more important than knowledge. For knowledge is limited, whereas imagination embraces the entire world, stimulating progress, and giving birth to evolution."* His ability to visualize abstract concepts was not just a quirk, but a powerful tool that unlocked the secrets of the universe.

The Transformative Power of Creative Visualization

Einstein's story serves as a compelling reminder of the transformative power of creative visualization. Whether you're tackling complex theories, planning innovative projects, or dreaming about your future, harnessing the power of imagination and vivid mental imagery can lead you to groundbreaking insights and accomplishments.

Visualization is a key part of mindfulness that can help with college success, and here's why: Visualization is a way to activate a positive intention. Imagine you're studying for a big exam or working on a challenging project. With visualization, you are able to picture yourself succeeding in these tasks—you activate your imagination by seeing yourself acing the exam or finishing the project with pride and appreciation. This mental picture can make you feel more confident and less stressed, and without you realizing, it is gently pulling you toward your desired outcome by making you more mindful. Visualization works hand in hand with mindfulness because it brings your focus to the present moment. When you visualize, you're not just daydreaming; you're actively engaging the electrical wiring in your brain to see, and experience, positive outcomes. This practice then makes the actual event feel familiar and manageable, which is something the brain finds comforting and rewarding.

Studies have shown that visualization can enhance performance in various fields, from sports to academics. One well-known study in the realm of sports psychology was conducted in the 1980s by Dr. Richard Suinn, a pioneer in sport psychology. He worked with Olympic athletes and found that when they visualized performing their sport, their muscle fibers fired in the same way as when they were physically practicing. This showed that mental rehearsal could effectively train the brain and muscles almost as if they were performing the activity.

In a similar study conducted by Dr. Alvaro Pascual-Leone, a neuroscientist at Harvard Medical School, participants were divided into two groups to learn a simple piece of music on the piano. One group physically practiced playing the piece on the piano for a set period each day. The other group didn't touch the piano at all but spent the same amount of time each day visualizing playing the piece, imagining the finger movements and hearing the music in their minds. After the practice period, both groups were tested on their ability to play the piece. Remarkably, the group that only visualized playing the piano showed almost the same

Visualization is a key part of mindfulness that can help with college success.

level of improvement as the group that physically practiced. Brain scans from the study showed that the same parts of the brain were activated in both groups, illustrating that mental practice could produce physical changes in the brain similar to those caused by physical practice.

These findings highlight the value of visualization for anyone looking to enhance their performance in any area, including college students. It shows that by mentally rehearsing tasks—whether it's giving a presentation, solving difficult problems, or even staying calm under pressure—students can improve their real-life performance and increase their confidence. Because findings show your brain does not distinguish between a real and an imagined activity, you can improve any skill by mentally rehearsing it. For you, visualizing studying, having a difficult conversation, preparing for an exam, or gearing up for a basketball game can be nearly as effective as physical practice, helping you boost your performance.

Further research has unveiled that the true secret to amplifying the power of your visualization lies in immersing yourself emotionally. The more deeply you engage with the joy, excitement, and satisfaction of your visualized experience, the more robust the chemical response in your brain and body becomes, optimizing your outcomes and overall impact. When you visualize a scenario vividly and with feeling, your brain experiences the unfolding of the imagined event as if it is happening, right now, in this moment. This illusion happens because of the way your brain processes emotions and distributes chemical signals throughout the body.

It's All in Your Mind

Let's look at several things that begin to happen physiologically when you engage your brain in the practice of visualization:

The Limbic System: When you visualize something, especially if it's emotionally charged, your limbic system (which includes the amygdala and hippocampus) gets activated. This part of the brain is responsible for emotional responses and memory. So if you're imagining acing a big exam or playing your best in a soccer game, your limbic system reacts as if the event is real.

Chemical Reactions: This mental imagery triggers the release of neurochemicals such as dopamine, serotonin, and endorphins. These chemicals are often associated with feelings of happiness, satisfaction, and motivation. This explains why visualizing a positive outcome can make you feel more motivated and optimistic.

Physiological Responses: These chemicals don't just stay in your brain; they are distributed throughout your body. For instance, if you're visualizing a stressful situation, your body might respond by releasing adrenaline, increasing your heart rate, and inducing a "fight or flight" response. Conversely, visualizing a calm and happy place can release relaxing chemicals, lowering your heart rate and reducing stress levels.

Muscle Memory: Remarkably, vivid visualization can even trigger muscle memory. Studies, like the one mentioned about piano players, show that mental practice can activate the same neural pathways as physical practice. This is why athletes use visualization to enhance their performance; they are not just imagining the sequence of actions, but they're also emotionally connecting with the experience, which further solidifies the memory.

Mind-Body Connection: Visualization bridges the mind-body connection by turning thoughts into physical sensations. When you imagine an event down to the sensory details—like the sight, sound, and even the feel of the situation—your body responds accordingly. This wholistic immersion makes the experience seem very real, strengthening your confidence and preparedness.

Visualization isn't just a daydreaming practice; it is a potent tool for emotional and mental preparation. By visualizing success, you can induce the emotional and physiological states associated with that success, effectively "rehearsing" those feelings and reactions. This can reduce anxiety, boost confidence, and enhance your overall performance when facing real challenges.

So the next time you're preparing for a big event—whether it is an exam, presentation, or athletic competition—take some time to vividly imagine yourself succeeding. Feel the pride, hear the applause, and sense the satisfaction. Your brain and body will respond as if you're already there, equipping you with the emotional readiness to turn that vision into reality.

The Power of Your Perception

After Tyler's transformative "moment of awakening" with Sam at the pond—where he resolved to intentionally steer his life in a more positive direction—he enrolled in my Mind Body Awareness course. Initially, he noticed a marked shift in his perspective, and his life began to reflect this newfound positivity . . . until the inevitable setbacks occurred.

He struggled to keep up during one hectic and stressful month during his semester, still balancing a part-time job, commuting to and from school, and taking a challenging course load. One class, in particular, was giving him a hard time: Advanced Physics, taught by Professor Donovan. Despite his best efforts, Tyler's grades in Professor Donovan's class were lackluster. He missed a few assignments, bombed a test, and received a terse email from the professor requesting a meeting to discuss his performance. From the moment he saw that email, Tyler's mind went into overdrive.

In his head, Tyler started to rehearse the impending meeting. He imagined every possible negative scenario, playing them over and over again like a broken tape. He saw himself walking into Professor Donovan's office, hearing the door click shut behind him. He could see the stern expression on the professor's face and hear the scathing tone in his voice. "You've been falling behind, Tyler," Professor Donovan would say. "This is unacceptable. How do you expect to pass this course with such poor grades? You're not putting in the effort. What's your excuse?"

Tyler played out his feeble responses in his mind, none of them satisfactory. "I'm sorry, Professor, I've had a lot on my plate." But in his mental rehearsals, nothing he said seemed good enough, leaving him feeling defeated. These mental responses no longer felt imagined, but instead felt very real, as if the scenario was truly happening every time he thought about it.

As the days passed, Tyler's anxiety grew. Ripples of panic stemmed from this constant mental movie, feeding his stress levels and keeping him up at night. His friends noticed the tension in his demeanor; he became withdrawn and snappy. The more he dwelled on the imagined confrontation, the more real it became. The anxiety he experienced in his body when he thought about the scenario with Professor Donovan persisted, even when he wasn't actively thinking about it.

This mounting anxiety also began to affect his performance in his other classes. One morning, after yet another sleepless night consumed by relentless worry, Tyler attempted to focus on his homework assignment for my class, which happened to be on visualization. It was in that moment it hit him: He had been using the power of visualization against himself. Instead of imagining success, he was visualizing and rehearsing worst-case scenarios on an endless loop. He realized he could shift his thinking, and therefore shift his feelings by imagining a more constructive conversation. It took a while for him to stop the well-rehearsed scenario and then reverse it to the positive, but with practice and consistency he succeeded at picturing himself confidently walking into Professor Donovan's office and giving an honest explanation for his struggles.

"Professor Donovan, I've been finding this class challenging, but I'm determined to improve. I want to understand where I'm going wrong and how I can do better."

In this new mental rehearsal, Professor Donovan wasn't scolding him but offering helpful advice. "I appreciate your honesty, Tyler. Let's work together to create a plan for you to catch up. Focus on your weak areas, and don't hesitate to ask for help during office hours."

Tyler made this revised visualization his new thought loop, which dramatically reduced his anxiety. When the day of the meeting finally came, he walked into Professor Donovan's office with a newfound sense of calm confidence. The conversation turned out to be constructive, just as he had visualized. Professor Donovan was firm but supportive, helping Tyler outline a plan to get back on track.

Through this experience, Tyler learned the profound impact of his thoughts and how redirecting his mental energy toward positive visualizations could change his outlook and reality. He continued to use this technique throughout his college career, turning potential stressors into opportunities for growth and success.

Let's Practice . . .

The Empowered Student Visualization

This practice guides you through powerful visualization steps, focusing on redirecting your thoughts to elevate confidence and empowerment. Envision yourself studying with energy, clarity, and focus. By fully immersing in the visualization, feeling the emotions, and seeing each action step vividly, you transform anxieties and negative patterns into empowering details. Ready to ignite your inner strength? Let's dive in together.

1. **Find a Quiet Space.** Sit comfortably in a quiet space where you won't be interrupted. Close your eyes and take three deep 5-Phase Breaths to center yourself.
2. **Set the Scene.** Imagine yourself walking into your favorite study spot—whether it's a cozy corner of the

library, a quiet coffee shop, or a sunny spot in the park. Feel the atmosphere around you: the gentle hum of background noise, the comfort of your chair, and perhaps the smell of coffee or fresh air.

3. **Visualize Success.** Picture yourself opening your laptop or notebook. See your to-do list in front of you, filled with tasks you need to accomplish. Visualize yourself effortlessly working through each task. You're focused and energized—every concept, every formula, and every bit of information comes to you with ease.

4. **Engage Your Senses.** As you work through your tasks, immerse yourself in the sensory details. Hear the soft tapping of your keyboard, feel the texture of the pages as you turn them, and see the neat, organized notes you're taking. Picture your surroundings—the warm glow of a study lamp, the stack of books beside you, the tranquil view outside the window.

5. **Incorporate Emotions.** Now feel the emotions tied to your success. Imagine the pride swelling within you as you complete each item on your to-do list. Feel the excitement as you understand a difficult concept fully. Sense the joy and relief as you see your progress. Let these positive emotions wash over you, reinforcing your ability to succeed.

6. **Visualize the Future.** Next, fast-forward to a moment in the near future when you've achieved your academic goals—maybe it's the day you ace an important exam, complete a major project, or receive your grades. Visualize yourself feeling the joy of focusing and dedicating your attention to your preparation and completion of the task. Let go of the outcome and instead feel the pride of your commitment and dedication.

7. **Affirm and Strengthen.** As you enjoy these moments, internally affirm your strengths and capabilities. Repeat to yourself, "I am capable and focused. I am achieving my academic goals. I handle challenges with ease."

8. **Return to the Present.** Slowly bring yourself back to the present moment by taking three deep 5-Phase Breaths. Feel the surface you're sitting on, hear the sounds around you . . . and now gently open your eyes. Carry the feelings of confidence, focus, and positivity with you.

Incorporating this visualization practice into your daily routine can equip you with the mental resilience and positive outlook needed to navigate college life successfully. Let yourself replicate this practice in all areas of your life. You might visualize enjoying a night out with friends or having a fun day at work. You can use this visualization to prepare for a job interview or a challenging conversation with your parents. You are limited only by your imagination!

Journal Prompts . . .

1. **Reflect on Your Visualization Experience:** Describe the favorite study spot that you visualized. What specific details made it a productive and comfortable place for you? Ask yourself, *"How do I imagine myself in this space feeling more focused and relaxed?"*

2. **Emotional Connection:** Think about the positive emotions you experienced during your visualization. How did feeling pride, joy, and excitement influence your outlook on your academic tasks? Ask yourself, *"How can I harness these emotions in real-life situations to boost my motivation and confidence?"*

3. **Future Success:** Picture a specific academic goal you have for this semester, such as acing an exam or completing a major project. Write a detailed account of achieving this goal, and ask yourself, *"How does this make me feel?"* . . .*"How do others respond to my success?"* *"What might be its impact on my confidence and future aspirations?"*

4. **Affirmations and Beliefs:** List three affirmations that resonate with you from the visualization exercise, such as "I am capable and focused," or "I handle challenges with ease." Reflect on why these affirmations are meaningful to you and ask yourself, *"How can these help me shape my mindset during stressful or challenging times?"*

5. **Strategies for Real-Life Application:** Based on your visualization, identify practical steps you can take to replicate the positive outcomes in your daily study routine. For instance, how can you create a study environment that mimics your visualized space? Ask yourself, *"What specific techniques (like deep breathing or positive self-talk) can I use to maintain focus and reduce stress?"*

After completing these journal prompts, take a moment to reflect on any patterns or insights that emerge. How can your visualization practice and the reflections from your journaling inform your approach to studying and handling academic challenges, athletic challenges, interview challenges, or anything else in your life? By regularly engaging with these prompts, you can deepen your self-awareness and strengthen your visualization technique, making it an even more effective tool for academic success and beyond.

Bringing It All Together

By incorporating the powerful tool of visualization into your daily routine, you take control of your thinking, redirecting it in to the direction of your choosing. This is one more step in taking ownership of your thoughts, your emotions, and your life. You *can* change your mind, your emotions, and your outcomes with mindful awareness, much like Tyler realized with the conversation with his professor. By engaging your emotions and vividly imagining outcomes that feel good, you can trigger the same mental and physiological responses as if you were experiencing these successes in the present moment. Reflecting on these visualizations through targeted journal prompts can further solidify your awareness, clarify your goals, and keep you focused on a positive trajectory. The practice not only reduces stress in the moment, but also enhances your ability to navigate your action steps with clarity and determination. Remember, the strength of your mind is an incredibly potent resource—by using visualization and journaling, you're equipping yourself with the tools to not only imagine success, but to achieve it!

Setting clear intentions and practicing visualizations aren't the only tools you can use to level up your success. As you continue along your mindfulness journey, your next step is to enjoy a magical focus that elevates life satisfaction—*gratitude*. In the next chapter, we explore the attitude of gratitude, uncovering how cultivating thankfulness can significantly enhance your academic performance, strengthen your relationships, and foster a more joyful college experience. Let's explore how cultivating gratitude can illuminate your path to deeper self-joy, which, of course, leads to greater success!

NINE

UNLEASHING THE POWER OF GRATITUDE

YOUR PATH TO FREEDOM AND EMPOWERMENT

Gratitude unlocks the fullness of life. It turns what we have into enough, and more. It turns denial into acceptance, chaos to order, confusion to clarity . . . it makes sense of our past, brings peace for today, and creates a vision for tomorrow.

—MELODY BEATTIE

As previously mentioned, Tyler's upbringing was fraught with challenges. Raised by a single mother alongside his two siblings in a neighborhood plagued by chaos, danger, and poverty, his circumstances were far from ideal. Sharing a bedroom with both siblings meant Tyler rarely had space or privacy, making it difficult even to collect his thoughts. Despite an inner conviction that he was destined for more, he struggled to envision a way out of this cycle.

When we introduced the module on cultivating an attitude of gratitude in class, Tyler was notably resistant. He candidly expressed that he found little in his life to be grateful for, listing the many stressors, injustices, and daily challenges he faced. His facial expression, crossed arms, and defensive posture all signaled that shifting his mindset would be no small feat.

Other students quickly joined the discussion, echoing Tyler's hesitations and sharing their own struggles. They spoke about the numerous challenges they faced, from a lack of money and constraints on their time, to the intense pressures exerted by demanding classes and professors. Additionally, they highlighted the overwhelming influence of social media and the expectations of their peer groups, all of which contributed to their resistance to adopting a gratitude mindset.

As the discussion continued, a palpable shift in the room occurred; the atmosphere grew tense, stressed, and somewhat agitated. This reaction is common when the focus turns to scarcity and lack, particularly in a setting where a group of individuals collectively shares and reinforces these feelings.

At this point, I invited the students to stand up, take a deep 5-Phase Breath, and begin shaking their bodies. We began with their hands and arms, then their hips and legs, then their spine and head, until the entire group of students was moving and grooving, from head to toe. I next encouraged them to visualize their tension as beads of water being shaken from their bodies, much like the droplets of water that fly off a wet dog when shaking itself dry after a dip in the pond (little did they know that this action has been proven to reduce cortisol levels, lower blood pressure, clear the mind, and increase circulation—all stress reducers). You

Stand up, inhale deeply, and imagine the tension dripping off you with each breath.

can also try this exercise: Stand up, inhale deeply, and begin shaking your body, imagining the tension dripping off you with each movement and each breath.

As the exercise progressed, I could see and feel the tension in the room begin to dissipate. Taking advantage of this newfound calm, I invited the students to find a comfortable seated or lying-down position. With their eyes closed, I guided them to focus inward, encouraging them to identify three to five aspects of their physical being for which they were grateful, such as acknowledging their effortless ability to breathe, their ability to walk to and from class, their gift of vision, their capacity to feel emotions, and their power to think, reason, and learn.

With this heightened awareness, the students, including Tyler, settled into a profound state of relaxation, evidenced by their stillness and open postures. Although they may not have realized it at the time, a significant chemical shift was occurring within their bodies. The release of dopamine, serotonin, and oxytocin—often referred to as the "feel-good hormones"—fostered a deep sense of ease and well-being. Simultaneously, their bodies began to reduce levels of cortisol—the stress hormone—further contributing to the overall sense of calm and relaxation they were experiencing. This biochemical shift not only eased their minds, but also promoted a more balanced and stress-free physiological state.

As the sense of ease continued to grow, I guided the students to explore other areas of their lives where they could identify sources of gratitude. I invited them to shine a spotlight on a particular gratitude they might have regarding their academic pursuits, financial status, friendships, jobs, families, and even their material possessions. Along the way, I reminded them to look beyond their unfulfilled expectations, lack of perfection, and comparison with others. I invited them to acknowledge what they have in the present moment.

Upon completing the exercise, we transitioned into a self-reflection discussion. The students shared their surprise at the profound mental and physical shift they experienced during the gratitude focus. Tyler, for instance, remarked, "I didn't realize just how grateful I am for my family and how much they support and encourage me. On the surface, I feel so annoyed by them and their noise, but beneath that, I recognize how much I love and appreciate them." His sentiment was met with nods of agreement from his classmates, who reflected similar newfound realizations of gratitude.

Perfection is not a precursor to gratitude; in fact, it is often a saboteur.

—ANONYMOUS

Pivot Your Perspective

Many people misunderstand gratitude, confusing it with the notion of needing to "have it all." A common mindset is, "I will be happy and grateful when I have _____"
—whether that blank is money, job success, an A in algebra, a boyfriend or girlfriend, etc. However, the essence of gratitude lies in appreciating what you currently have rather than waiting for some future state of having it all, which is captured so eloquently in a passage by Alfred D. Souza:

> For a long time it had seemed to me that life was about to begin—real life. But there was always some obstacle in the way, something to be gotten through first, some unfinished business, time still to be served, a debt to be paid. Then life would begin. At last it dawned on me that these obstacles were my life. This perspective has helped me to see there is no way to happiness. Happiness is the way. So, treasure every moment that you have. And treasure it more because you shared it with someone special, special enough to

spend your time with. And remember that time waits for no one.

So, stop waiting until you finish school, until you go back to school,
until you lose ten pounds, until you gain ten pounds,
until you have kids, until your kids leave the house,
until you start work, until you retire,
until you get married, until you get divorced,
until Friday night, until Sunday morning,
until you get a new car or home, until your car or home is paid off,
until spring, until summer, until fall, until winter,
until the first or fifteenth,
until your song comes on,
until you've had a drink, until you've sobered up,
until you die, until you are born again
to decide that there is no better time than right now to be happy.
Happiness is a journey, not a destination.

Gratitide is recognizing and appreciating the small, often overlooked, blessings and moments of joy in your daily life.

This passage richly illustrates the importance of embracing gratitude and finding happiness in what you already have, rather than wishing, hoping, and postponing gratitude and joy for some future time.

Developing an attitude of gratitude requires a significant shift in perspective. While it does involve acknowledging the good things in life, it is also about changing the way you perceive your experiences and circumstances. Instead of focusing on what you lack or what's going wrong (from a "scarcity mindset"), you begin paying attention to what you already have and what's going right (from an "abundance mindset"). This transformation involves recognizing and appreciating the small, often overlooked, blessings and moments of joy in your daily life. By actively choosing to focus on these positives, you are training your mind to see the abundance around you, leading to a more fulfilling and contented outlook on life.

It's a common experience to find ourselves dwelling on the negative rather than the positive aspects of life, which might make you ask, "Why is it so easy to focus on the negative?" This tendency isn't just a matter of personal disposition—it's deeply rooted in the structure and function of our brains.

Master Your Neurobiology

Let's take a look at this from the perspective of neurobiology (the scientific study of the nervous system, including brain function and its connection to behaviors, thoughts, and emotions).

The Role of the Reptilian Brain: The reptilian brain, also known as the *basal ganglia*, is the oldest part of the human brain in evolutionary terms. This brain region is responsible for our most primal survival functions, such as regulating heart rate, breathing, and the fight-or-flight response. Its primary focus is on keeping us safe and ensuring our survival.

Survival Mechanisms and Negativity: From an evolutionary perspective, our ancestors had to be acutely aware of potential threats and dangers in order to survive. Whether it was a predator lurking nearby or a sudden environmental change, being able to quickly assess and react to threats was crucial. This constant vigilance led to the development of what psychologists call a "negativity bias."

Negativity Bias: Negativity bias refers to our brain's predisposition to prioritize negative information over positive information. This bias means that we are more likely to notice, remember, and dwell on something negative. The reptilian brain plays a significant role in this process because it is wired to focus on potential threats. This focus ensures we remain alert to dangers that could jeopardize our safety and well-being.

Fight-or-Flight Response: When we encounter a perceived threat, the reptilian brain activates the fight-or-flight response. This response floods our bodies with stress hormones—such as cortisol and adrenaline—preparing us to either confront or flee from the danger. While this response is essential for short-term survival, it can be detrimental to our emotional well-being when it becomes a chronic state.

Modern Stressors: In today's world, the threats we face are rarely life-threatening predators. Instead, they manifest as stressors from exams, social pressures, financial worries, and countless other forms of modern anxiety. However, our brains still react to these stressors with the same intensity as if we were facing immediate physical danger. As a result, we find it easy to focus on what's wrong or what might go wrong, often at the expense of recognizing what's going well.

In contrast to our predecessors—who, after escaping life-threatening predators, would relax, thus allowing their cortisol levels to return to normal—our current lifestyles keep us in a state of constant stress, whether perceived or real. Activities such as constant pursuing scrolling, instant, access to information; engaging with blue-screen activities like gaming, social media, and television; combined with perceived pressures to "keep up with the Instagrammers," all keep our cortisol levels elevated. This continuous, elevated state of stress prevents our physiological systems from returning to a baseline of calm, creating an environment where anxiety and negativity can thrive unchecked.

However, there is good news! There is a part of the brain that can override the reptilian brain. This is called the prefrontal cortex. The prefrontal cortex is the region of the brain responsible for higher cognitive functioning, such as decision-making, reasoning, problem-solving, and regulating emotions. It is crucial in moderating behaviors and responses that originate from the more primitive parts of the brain, like the reptilian brain and the amygdala. While it is not completely developed until your mid-twenties, some practices strengthen your prefrontal cortex at any age. I bet you can already guess what some of those practices are based on our previous discussions. Here are the top four:

- Gratitude
- Mindfulness
- Meditation
- Self-reflection

Gratitude exercises can help counteract your brain's negativity bias by training your mind to focus on positive aspects of your life. Understanding the neurobiological basis of your focus on negativity can help you appreciate the importance of practices such as gratitude. Over time, this practice can help to physically rewire your brain, making it easier to notice and appreciate the good, even when faced with challenges.

By acknowledging the influence of your reptilian brain and its negativity bias, you gain insight into why it's so effortless to focus on the negative. This awareness empowers you to more actively cultivate gratitude and positivity, enabling you to navigate life's challenges with a more balanced and resilient mindset. Developing this shift in perspective requires awareness, practice, and repetition, but the rewards are well worth the effort. Over time, you'll experience greater ease and relaxation, as well as an elevated trust in life.

Let's take a look at how you can shift your perspective (focus) by intentionally elevating your reptilian brain's thought pattern to a prefrontal-cortex thought pattern. Notice how a shift in perspective changes the feel of each experience.

Reptilian Brain Thought (stress hormones)	Prefrontal Cortex Thought (happy hormones)
Ugh . . . I have to pay my electric bill.	*I am grateful for my electric bill because it means I stay warm and have light at night.* **I feel safe.**
I have to clean all these dishes.	*I am grateful for the dirty dishes after this fun party with all my friends.* **I feel connected.**
I have to do my laundry again.	*I am grateful for the dirty laundry because it means I have clothes to wear.* **I feel abundant.**
I hate the morning alarm.	*I am grateful the alarm went off this morning because it means I have a reason to get up and something to pursue.* **I feel of value.**
I dread having to pay rent again.	*I am grateful for my rent because it means I have a home to live in.* **I feel secure.**
Ugh . . . another day at the job.	*I am grateful I get to work today because it means I have the opportunity to earn money, meet my needs, and have some fun.* **I feel purposeful.**

These true-to-life examples show how a simple shift in perspective can transform mundane or challenging tasks into opportunities for gratitude. By focusing on the underlying positives in your daily activities, you can cultivate a sense of appreciation that enriches your life. With the higher-functioning contributions from your prefrontal cortex, you are capable of shifting your perspective from the negative, stress-inducing thoughts to the positive, ease-inducing thoughts. It is only a choice away. The thought you feed the most will become the driving force in your life, as illustrated by this Native American parable:

An old Cherokee grandfather was talking with his grandson.

He said, "My son, there is a battle between two wolves inside us all. One is evil. It is anger, envy, greed, arrogance, resentment, lies, and ego. The other is good. It is joy, peace, love, hope, humility, kindness, empathy, and truth."

The grandson thought about it for a minute and then asked his grandfather, "Which wolf wins?"

The grandfather simply replied, "The one you choose to feed."

Let's Practice . . .

Spotlighting Gratitude
This practice offers a refreshing pause, allowing you to shift your focus from what you lack to what you have. By slowing down and acknowledging all that you have, you will cultivate a mindset of abundance and joy. Ready to transform your perspective and embrace a more grateful heart? Let's practice.

1. Close your eyes. Take three deep 5-Phase Breaths. Let your shoulders drop and your back relax. Feel the support beneath you.

2. Identify **five things you are grateful for in this moment.** Nothing is too small to acknowledge. This could be the breath you are breathing, the chair you are sitting on, the laptop you own, or the shirt you are wearing.

3. Take a deep 5-Phase Breath and bring your attention to **five things you are grateful for that happened today.** This might be having received a smile from a stranger, the temperature outside, the assignment you completed, or the paycheck you received.

   Note: The reptilian brain might jump in and say something like, "Yeah, but who cares about the stranger? I'd rather have a smile from _____," or "The temperature could be better," or "I should've spent more time on the assignment," or "My wish the paycheck was bigger." If/when this happens, take a deep breath and speak to the reptilian brain like it is a separate entity. This might sound like, "I hear you, reptilian brain, but you get to take a rest because I am choosing high-level thoughts right now, and I choose gratitude for what I have."

4. Take a deep 5-Phase Breath and bring your attention to **five things you are grateful for in life.** This might be the journey you are currently on, the support you've received from family, the friends you have, or your overall health and motivation. Let yourself get lost in all there is to be grateful for, which is always just a thought away.

5. Stay in this process for as long as it feels good. Practice bringing your attention and focus back to gratitude, no matter what comes up in your mind. When the reptilian brain pops in, distracting you with negative thoughts, simply continue breathing and return to gratitude. This, indeed, is part of the practice.

6. When you feel complete and are ready to return, take three deep 5-Phase Breaths, bringing yourself back a little more with each breath. As you are doing this, notice your mind and body. How are you feeling? How is this similar to or different from when you started?

Be grateful for what you already have while you pursue your goals. If you aren't grateful for what you already have, what makes you think you would be happy with more?

—OPRAH WINFREY

Journal Prompts . . .

1. When I began the Spotlighting Gratitude Practice, I was feeling and thinking . . . After the Practice, I'm now feeling and thinking . . .

2. Create a list of ten things you are grateful for. These can range from current comforts, like a safe home and soft pillows, to relationships that lift you up, to material possessions and the ability to think independently. Remember, nothing is too small to notice. Take a deep breath and add ten more. Let your list expand to one hundred things you are grateful for. It's okay to build out this list over the next couple of days.

3. Call to mind a thought you have that feels heavy, negative, or stress-inducing, such as "I have so much homework to do" or "my car broke down again," etc. Then take a deep breath to activate your prefrontal cortex

and create a high-level gratitude for that same thought. For example, "I have homework to do" could shift to "I am so thankful I get to attend college."

Bringing It All Together

Embracing gratitude can change your life, shifting your perspective from what's missing to appreciating what you already have. We discussed how our brains naturally focus on the negative—thanks to the reptilian brain—but you can override this by engaging your prefrontal cortex through mindfulness. Simple practices, such as standing up, shaking off tension, and visualizing stress slipping away like droplets of water, can make a big difference. Daily exercises like shifting your attention to high-level thinking—such as looking beyond the negative thought to a positive outcome—help you uncover hidden treasures of gratitude in your everyday routine and train your brain to think differently.

Remember the parable of the two wolves? The one you feed is the one that wins. By nurturing gratitude, you trigger feel-good hormones—like dopamine, serotonin, and oxytocin—while lowering stress-inducing cortisol. It's not about having it all; it's about appreciating what you have right now. So keep harvesting those blessings, cultivating a life full of thankfulness, mindfulness, and awareness. It's the new cool thing to do!

With the transformative practices of meditation, visualization, and gratitude now in your treasure chest, your next chapter explores how the great outdoors naturally relaxes your body, clears your mind, and refreshes your spirit. Discover simple ways to immerse yourself in nature and reconnect. Let's dive in and embrace the healing power of the natural world together.

TEN

GROUNDING YOURSELF IN NATURE

YOUR NATURAL PATH TO ZEN

And into the forest I go, to lose my mind and find my soul.

—JOHN MUIR

Kati, a recent UCLA graduate, was thrilled to move to the big city of New York. She was eager to soak up the energy of the bustling crowds, stroll through the shadows of towering skyscrapers, and immerse herself in the sounds of urban life. She thrived on the fast-paced energy of city living, moving from one project to the next with barely a moment to rest. Her days were spent in concrete buildings and under fluorescent lights, with the constant hum of traffic and city noise as her backdrop. But over time, she began to notice changes in her mood and health.

Kati found herself feeling increasingly anxious and stressed. She had trouble sleeping, often waking up in the middle of the night with a racing mind. Her energy levels plummeted, and she started experiencing frequent headaches. Trying to keep up with her demanding schedule, she turned to caffeine and energy drinks, which only exacerbated her sleeplessness and irritability.

One weekend, feeling utterly drained, Kati decided to visit her friend's hometown in upstate New York. It had been years since she had visited this quiet town where she'd spent summers hanging out with her childhood friend. Upon her arrival, she immediately felt a sense of calm wash over her as she took in the lush greenery and the sound of birds chirping.

The next morning, Kati went for a walk in the nearby forest. Feeling the sun on her face and the earth beneath her feet, she realized just how much she had missed being in nature. She paused by a serene river, listening to the gentle flow of water and the rustling of leaves in the breeze. For the first time in months, she took a deep breath and felt her anxiety begin to melt away.

Over the next few days in the countryside, Kati noticed a significant improvement in her mood and overall well-being. Her headaches disappeared, she slept soundly, and she felt more energized and clearheaded than she had in a long time. She realized that her urban lifestyle, devoid of natural interactions, had been taking a serious toll on her mental and physical health. This had happened slowly over time, so she did not immediately make the connection.

Back in the city, Kati made a conscious effort to incorporate nature into her daily routine. She started taking weekend trips to nearby parks, kept a small garden on her apartment balcony, and opted for scenic walking routes instead of taking the subway to work. She chose to join a local community gardening group. She felt grounded with her hands in the dirt and connected while tending to the plants.

The changes were profound and lasting. Kati's anxiety decreased, her sleep improved, and she felt a renewed sense of balance and happiness. She understood that her connection with nature was not just a luxury, but a crucial component of her health and well-being.

Kati's story is a reminder that our natural surroundings are essential to our mental and physical health. In the hustle and bustle of modern life, it's easy to lose touch with nature, but as Kati discovered, rekindling this essential connection can lead to profound rejuvenation and wholistic health.

Born of the Earth

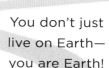

You don't just live on Earth— you are Earth!

Connecting with nature can be a game-changer for feeling inner peace and a deeper connection with self and others. It's fascinating to see how deeply intertwined humans are with the natural world, often in ways we might not fully recognize. Consider for a moment: You are composed of 84 minerals, 23 elements, and eight gallons of water, all distributed among 38 billion cells. From the Earth's raw materials, you were meticulously crafted, guided by a genetic blueprint contained in a double helix so tiny it fits within a sperm cell. Consider this: You are formed from the recycled essence of butterflies, plants, rocks, streams, firewood, wolf skins, and shark teeth. These elements are broken down to the smallest of particles and reconstituted into the most complex living organism on our planet. To disconnect from Earth, you are disconnecting from the very umbilical cord that sustains, nourishes, and helps you thrive. You don't just live on Earth—you are Earth!

This helps explain our innate desire to venture outdoors, immerse ourselves in nature, feel the sunlight on our faces, touch water, observe the moon cycles, float down rivers, climb mountains, feel the breeze, stand in the shade, hug trees, and marvel at birds flying above.

We find inner peace as we watch the waves roll to shore and ebb away. We feel mesmerized while observing a rainbow or the flames of a campfire as they swirl and dance in magnificent oranges, reds, blues, and purple. We are drawn into a state of wonder and contemplation while stargazing, feeling small and also connected to the Universe. We melt into ease while petting a dog or cat. We sink into relaxation while grooming a horse.

The science that studies humans' innate affinity for nature is called *biophilia*, which literally translated means, "a love of life or living things." Biophilia is a fascinating topic, and it taps in to our inherent inclination to seek connections with nature and other forms of life. This concept extends to various environments—urban, rural, and even virtual spaces. It suggests that our health, well-being, and ability to thrive are deeply tied to our relationship with the natural world. The term *biophilia* was popularized by biologist Edward O. Wilson in his groundbreaking book, not surprisingly titled *Biophilia*. In it, he proposes that humans possess not just a natural affinity for living systems, but also an intrinsic need to connect with them. Here are a few interesting aspects and surprising studies related to biophilia:

Improved Cognitive Function and Well-Being. A study by Rachel and Stephen Kaplan (1995) introduced the Attention Restoration Theory (ART), which posits that exposure to natural environments can help restore depleted cognitive resources. Their research found that spending time in or viewing nature can improve focus, memory, and cognitive performance. Students experiencing mental fatigue showed significant improvement in cognitive function after a brief walk in a natural setting compared to those who walked in urban settings.[3]

Stress Reduction. A study conducted in Japan found that spending time in a forest environment can significantly lower cortisol levels (a hormone associated with stress), lower blood pressure, and inhibit depression, improve mood, enhance cognitive function, and even boost the immune system.

The practice known as *Shinrin-yoku*, or "forest bathing," has shown profound impacts on stress reduction and overall physical health. It's a simple yet profound way to reconnect with nature, grounding us in the present moment and promoting a sense of calm and clarity. In return, as we gain more from these experiences, we become advocates for preserving these natural spaces against urban encroachment and environmental degradation.[4]

Revitalization. Often, the constant demands of being a student and juggling many different roles can leave you feeling drained and out of energy. The practice of "earthing," also known as "grounding," has been found to recharge your body. This practice involves direct physical contact with the Earth's surface, such as walking barefoot on grass, sand, or soil. The transfer of electrons from the Earth into your skin can help neutralize free radicals and reduce inflammation. The grounding effect can also promote better sleep, alleviate chronic pain, and improve energy levels. A study published in the *Journal of Environmental and Public Health* found that grounding can significantly enhance overall well-being by balancing the body's electrical energy and stabilizing your natural rhythms. With such compelling evidence, earthing offers a simple yet powerful way to reconnect with nature and recharge your physical and emotional health.

Biophilic design and well-being. Research shows that incorporating nature, such as indoor plants, natural light, and water features, into our living and working spaces significantly reduces stress, enhances mood, and boosts overall well-being. Imagine a campus library filled with greenery or a park beside your residence hall. These nurturing spaces promote mental and emotional health and were added with intention. The presence of nature isn't just visually pleasing; it also induces a chemical shift in the mind and body, leading to a sense of calm, greater ease, and clearer thinking.[5]

Healing Power of Animals. Hanging out with animals—whether it's petting a dog, watching fish swim, or just listening to birds sing—has been proven to cut stress, lower blood pressure, and even chase away loneliness. Just having animals around us every day can make a difference, filling our lives with peace and connection. It has even been shown that oxytocin, serotonin, dopamine, and endorphins are all released while petting a dog or cat.

I'm sure you've experienced coming home after a rough day, being greeted by an affectionate dog or cat, and after chilling with them for just a few moments, feeling a sense of ease and comfort. Whether it's your dog greeting you at the door or your cat curling up on your lap, these moments help you unwind and stay grounded. Animals remind you to enjoy the little things and be present in the moment.

Animals also shine in more structured therapeutic roles. From hospitals to universities, therapy animals bring emotional support right where it's needed most. Consider the miniature horse, Mystic, who visits hospitals and nursing homes, comforting patients with her sweet presence. And Ricochet, a talented golden retriever, who found her calling surfing with people with disabilities, wounded veterans, and kids with special needs. Her company not only helps with physical therapy, but also boosts confidence and emotional health.

The benefits of being around animals go far beyond any specific setting. Daily interactions with pets and service animals push us toward conservation and advocacy, making sure our furry, feathered, and finned friends get the love and care they deserve, which also increases our sense of connection. So, whether it's cuddling with your cat, watching fish swim, or meeting a therapy animal, these relationships are enriching. They help us stay calm, happy, and connected. Plus, they remind us of life's simple joys, urging us to appreciate and protect the wonderful creatures who give us so much.

Another surprising and powerful realization is that the connections we cultivate with nature and animals are not one-sided. When we embrace these relationships, we not only nurture our own well-being, but we also nurture their well-being. Plants thrive when in the presence of humans. Animals experience an influx of serotonin (the happy hormone) when being petted and hugged. We become guardians of one

> Animals remind you to enjoy the little things and be present in the moment.

another. By prioritizing green spaces and protecting wildlife, we're advocating for the entire ecosystem's health, which elevates the quality of life for us all. In essence, the more we realize and honor the profound connections we share with nature and animals, the more we create a life imbued with mindfulness, inner peace, and a sustainable, respectful coexistence.

The Power of Nature's Reset

Meet Erin, a junior at CU Boulder. Like many students, she felt perpetually overwhelmed by the relentless pressure of academic responsibilities. One particularly hectic day, she inadvertently discovered the power of nature's reset. Finding herself near the creek that meanders through the heart of Boulder, she felt a magnetic pull to sit along its edge. The symphony of flowing water seemed to call her, inviting her to rest and reflect. She chose a comfortable rock, settled in, and allowed her senses to take over. She focused on what she could see and then closed her eyes. She shifted her focus to what she could hear and then smell and then taste and then feel. She absorbed it all.

With each breath, Erin felt her burdens easing, her worries and anxieties flowing away with the current. The creek's resilience reminded her of her own inner strength. She realized that just like the water smoothly flowing around obstacles, she could navigate and overcome the challenges in her way with ease, grace and flow. At first, she thought the creek was teaching her resilience, but in her next breath it dawned on her; the creek was simply reminding her of her own inherent resilience. She had only temporarily lost sight of it during the chaos of her semester. Reflecting on her experience, Erin said, "It felt like I was hitting a reset button. As my entire mind and body let go, there was space for me to reconnect with my inner strength, confidence, and knowing." She then "threw" her chaotic energy, which she had been carrying with her for weeks, into the creek and watched it float away. This somatic exercise (going through the body motion of throwing something into the water) elevated her sensation of "letting it all go." As she wrapped up her session by the creek, she was filled with an overwhelming feeling of lightness and a sense of gratitude—gratitude for the creek, the rocks, the trees, the birds, her body, and for her whole Self.

Just as Tyler and Sam found a sense of deeper peace near the pond during their reflective conversations, and Kati was able to reset her soul by visiting the countryside, Erin was also discovering the profound benefits of nature—an endless well of energy, clarity, ease, and connection that's often overlooked in the chaos and hustle of daily life.

You should sit in nature twenty minutes a day.
Unless you're busy, then sit there for an hour.

—DR. SUKHRAJ DHILLON

Simple Nature Practices

The key is to make time in nature a consistent part of your routine. Think of it like a vitamin. You take vitamins to strengthen your systems—immune, respiratory, digestive, muscular, and so on. This builds over time, not just from a single dose. Similarly, the benefits of a nature practice accumulate with every session, filling you up and fortifying you along the way. While you'll certainly feel immediate benefits, nature time helps to buffer your systems against the stress and chaos of daily life over the long haul. While the goal is to be outside for at least twenty minutes per day, never pass up an opportunity to step outside, even if for only a few minutes throughout the day.

Whether it's through daily small doses or longer weekend immersions, regular interaction with nature can improve your mood, reduce stress, and enhance your overall well-being. Even in a bustling city like New York, there are plenty of opportunities to connect with nature if you make it a priority. From Central Park to community gardens, finding your own slice of green space can make a huge difference in your life.

Here are some easy and empowering ideas to activate your natural connection.

DAILY ACTIVITIES

Soul Stroll: Begin your day with a mindful walk dedicated to simply engaging all of your senses and none of your thinking. Imagine awakening your soul and inviting it into your day with you.

Campus Walk: Park your car away from campus and walk to school. Use this time to connect with your breath and the happenings around you. Disconnect from all distractions, such as electronics, book-reading (yes, I have seen people walk and read at the same time), or thinking about classes.

Lunchtime Fiesta: Rather than sitting in the stuffy cafeteria during lunchtime, take your lunch outside to a green space or courtyard. Soak in the sounds of the birds and the beauty of the surroundings while you are savoring your lunch.

WEEKEND ADVENTURES

Nature Trails: Dedicate a few hours on weekends to hike on local trails, visit natural reserves, or walk through a sunflower field. Prepping for the adventure can even be fun and mindful as you pack your favorite snacks, beverages, and picnic blanket.

Day Trips: Plan day trips to the beach, mountains, or countryside to immerse yourself in different natural settings. Consider turning off the radio and listening to the hum of the engine, the turning of the wheels, and the air whooshing by your window. Try a back road you haven't been on before. Watch for unusual sitings, such as abandoned miner cabins or swirly dunes.

Incorporate Nature into Your Environment

Garden or Balcony Plants: Grow a small garden or keep plants on your balcony or in your room. Tending to plants can be very therapeutic, and they are great for filtering the air you breathe.

Outdoor Workspaces: If possible, work or study outside for a change of scenery, fresh air, and nature sounds, such as birds, squirrels, and if you're lucky, a running stream.

Outdoor Activities

Cycling and/or Running: Go for bike rides or runs through parks or along scenic routes instead of in an indoor fitness center.

Picnics and Barbecues: Organize your next family or friend gathering at a picnic site. Include some fun games so everybody stays active.

SPECIFIC MINDFULNESS NATURE TECHNIQUES

- **Nature Meditation:** Practice meditation or mindfulness exercises such as yoga, Tai Chi, and meditation in a green space, on a trail, or near a stream.

- **Earthing:** Walk barefoot, or lie down, on natural surfaces like grass, sand, or soil, absorbing the natural electrical charge.

- **Forest Bathing:** Practice *Shinrin-yoku*, or forest bathing, by mindfully walking, sitting, or meditating in a forest.

- **Skygazing:** Take a few minutes each day to look up at the sky, whether it's during sunrise, sunset, moonrise, or moonset. Or you could simply cloud-watch. Just simply look up.

INDOOR PRACTICES

You might be reading this while sitting warm and cozy inside on a ten-degree day, watching the snow swirl outside, and wondering how you're going to get your serotonin boost from Mother Nature. While indoor alternatives might seem less powerful than being outside, studies have shown they can still have a significant impact on your nervous system. Let's give these a try:

- **Indoor Plants:** Adding houseplants into your living space not only infuses greenery and vitality into an otherwise plain interior, but it also supports and stabilizes your intricate nervous system.

- **Nature Videos**: Nature documentaries or YouTube videos showcasing beautiful landscapes and wildlife can create a decrease in cortisol (a stress hormone) and an increase in serotonin (a happy hormone).

Listen to Nature Soundtracks: Sounds like rain, forest ambiance, ocean waves, and bird songs can regulate the vagus nerve, which is responsible for creating the relaxation response.

Virtual Nature Tours: Explore virtual tours of national parks, botanical gardens, and natural wonders online. Many websites and apps offer immersive experiences that make you feel like you're exploring the great outdoors. Remember, the mind does not know the difference between what is happening in the moment and what you are telling it is happening, so the same positive chemical responses will be elicited while watching the immersive experience without literally being there.

Nature Art and Photography: Decorate your space with nature-themed artwork or photography. Images of forests, mountains, and oceans can help bring the outdoors inside and create a tranquil atmosphere.

Aromatherapy: Use essential oils derived from plants, such as lavender, eucalyptus, or pine, to evoke the scents of nature. Diffusing these oils can help create a soothing, natural environment indoors.

Indoor Water Features: Set up a small indoor fountain or water feature. The sound of flowing water can be incredibly relaxing and reminiscent of time spent outdoors by a stream or river.

Imagine the transformative impact of incorporating these simple nature practices into your daily routine. You don't need to do them all—just choose the ones that fit into your life today. Stay in tune with what your mind and body need. Some days, when the demands are higher, you might benefit from a little extra nature practice. On other days, perhaps some calming bird sounds and a nature picture will suffice. By being aware and intentional, you walk the natural path to Zen with ease, grounded in a profound sense of calm. This calmness translates into better focus, improved memory, and enhanced problem-solving skills—a powerful tool for not only your studies but all areas of your life.

Let's Practice . . .

Daily Nature Pause

This is a great time to step outside, away from screens and schedules, and immerse yourself in the tranquility of nature. This nature practice invites you to pause and reconnect with the natural world. Ready to experience the calming embrace of the outdoors? Let's embark on this peaceful journey together.

1. **Find Your Spot.** Choose a quiet spot outdoors where you feel comfortable, whether it's a nearby park, your backyard, or a balcony. If going outside isn't an option, sit near a window with a view of nature or next to a plant, and play a recording of nature sounds (like birdsong or flowing water).

2. **Get Comfortable.** Sit or stand in a relaxed position. Take a moment to adjust your posture, ensuring you're comfortable. Close your eyes if you feel comfortable doing so, or keep them softly focused on a natural element (a tree, a flower, etc.).

3. **Deep Breathing.** Begin with three, deep 5-Phase Breaths. Inhale slowly through your nose, hold for a moment, and then exhale slowly through your mouth. Repeat this deep, mindful breathing for a few cycles to center yourself.

4. **Engage Your Senses.** Spend the next few minutes focusing on one sense at a time.

- **Sight:** Observe the colors, shapes, and movements around you. Notice the details in leaves, flowers, or the sky.
- **Sound:** Listen attentively to the sounds of nature. Focus on birds chirping, leaves rustling, or any other natural noises.
- **Touch:** If possible, touch a natural object like a leaf, a rock, or tree bark. Notice its texture, temperature, and feel.
- **Smell:** Take a moment to breathe in the scents around you. Pay attention to the fresh air, soil, flowers, or any natural smells.

5. **Mindful Reflection.** Take a few minutes to reflect on how you feel in this moment. Notice any changes in your mood or stress levels. Allow yourself to simply be present without any judgments or expectations.

6. **Express Gratitude.** Conclude your practice by silently expressing gratitude for the natural elements around you, the time you've taken for yourself, and the calmness you feel. You can also think of something specific you're grateful for in your life today.

7. **Slow Transition.** Slowly bring your awareness back to your surroundings, while completing three 5-Phase Breaths. On your final deep breath, stretch gently, slowly opening your eyes. Invite yourself to carry this sense of peace with you as you transition into your daily activities.

Journal Prompts . . .

1. **Describe Your Experience:** Reflect on today's Daily Nature Pause. What did you notice about your surroundings? How did the sights, sounds, scents, and textures of nature influence your mood and thoughts? Write about any moments that stood out to you and how you felt before and after the practice.

2. **Mindfulness and Presence:** Consider how the practice helped you engage with the present moment. Did you find it challenging or easy to stay focused on your senses? Write about any distractions that arose and how you dealt with them. How does this compare to other mindfulness practices you've tried?

3. **Personal Reflections and Gratitude:** Reflect on any feelings of gratitude or emotional shifts you experienced during the Daily Nature Pause. Did any specific parts of the practice make you feel particularly grateful or peaceful? Write about how this practice might have impacted your overall sense of well-being, and consider how you can integrate similar moments of connecting to nature into your daily life.

Bringing It All Together

Imagine transforming your life by embracing this "natural path to Zen." Throughout this chapter, you've uncovered the incredible power of reconnecting with nature to boost your well-being and awaken your mindfulness. We started by diving into your innate desire to engage with the natural world, supported by eye-opening studies that reveal how such interactions can reduce stress, sharpen your mind, and flood your spirit with peace. We've mapped out exciting ways to weave nature into your daily routine, even if you're navigating the urban jungle or battling wintry weather—from energizing daily walks and nurturing indoor plants, to exploring virtual nature tours and basking in the soothing sounds of water and birdsong.

By making these mindful nature practices a regular part of your routine, you're not just adding moments of tranquility, you're engaging in a complete lifestyle shift that nurtures your inner peace by walking a natural path to Zen.

WELCOME
TO THE FINAL LEG
OF YOUR
MINDFULNESS
JOURNEY!

Practicing mindfulness consistently provides a resilient foundation,
so we don't have to wait for stress to seize its benefits.

—TARA BRACH

Ah . . . what an extraordinary journey you have been on! You have not only established a deeply rooted foundation, but you have also ascended the paths to the summit, mastering intention setting, meditation, guided visualization, gratitude, and reconnecting with nature.

Your foundations, like the robust roots of a mighty tree, will support and provide you with immense strength and resilience. Meanwhile, your practices, resembling the well-trodden paths up a mountain, guide you toward your highest potential.

Now you have arrived at a pivotal point in your journey, where you can elevate your mindful focus by truly living it.

In Part Three, you will delve into the unique challenges presented by the twenty-first century, understanding what sets this era apart from all others. You will also embark on challenges designed to seamlessly integrate mindfulness into your daily life, empowering you to ward off stress and anxiety before they even arise.

So, dive in when you're ready—and relish the experience of putting your newfound awareness and practices into dynamic action.

Let's continue this exhilarating journey together!

Relish the experience of putting your newfound awareness and practices into dynamic action.

PART 3

ACTIVELY
ILLUMINATING
ZEN

ELEVEN

MINDFULNESS UNINTERRUPTED

NAVIGATING MODERN-DAY TECHNOLOGY

Often it happens that we live our lives in chains . . .
and we never even know we have the key.

—THE EAGLES

Over the past three decades, daily life has changed dramatically, in fact, more so than in any other thirty-year period of time—all due to technological advancements. That means in a single generation (typically a thirty-year period), the exponential growth in technology and connectivity has reshaped our world at a rate previous generations never experienced. The speed, breadth, and depth of these changes are unparalleled, fundamentally altering how we live, work, and interact.

To illustrate this profound shift, let's explore a day in the life of a college student from three different eras—Matt in 1990, Annette in 2005, and Tyler in 2020—to shed light on how technology has intricately woven itself into the very fabric of our existence.

Matt, a 20-year-old college student in 1990

Matt wakes up to the reliable buzz of his digital-display clock, shaking off sleep, and steps into the shower before starting his day. He grabs a quick bite to eat in the dorm cafeteria, free of electronic influences such as TVs, phones, or headsets, before hopping on his bike to ride across campus to his first class. On his way, he enjoys the crisp morning air and the quiet streets, a peaceful start to his busy day. He diligently takes notes in class with pen and paper, requiring him to be fully present and engaged as he exchanges thoughts and ideas with his peers. Later, Matt meets his friends for lunch in the bustling cafeteria, where they discuss homework, upcoming exams, and weekend plans, free from the pull of digital screens. Afterward, he heads to the library, where he spends hours poring over physical books and taking notes in preparation for his assignments. Come evening, Matt meets his friends for dinner in the cafeteria for another undisturbed, screen-free occasion that strengthens their bond. He's anticipating a call from a friend, so he heads back to his dorm and waits patiently by the landline (a phone that is physically connected to the wall). During the call, they excitedly hash out their weekend plans, settling on a spot and time to meet, comforted by the fact that there's no easy way to change or inform others of any updates. With their plans locked in, Matt dives back into his studies, tapping away on his typewriter to finish his reports. As the evening winds down, he settles into a good book, feeling relaxed and calm within his offline world, oblivious to the impending arrival of a "plugged-in" future. Satisfied and at peace, he tucks into bed around 10:30 p.m.

Annette, a 20-year-old college student in 2005

Annette wakes to music from her CD player/radio-alarm clock, and quickly checks her messages on her BlackBerry, before briefly joining her roommates in the kitchen. With a bowl of cereal in hand, she catches the morning news on TV, complete with a scrolling digital ticker at the bottom of the screen, making sure she is inundated with news from around the world. She then grabs her Discman (a portable CD player), plugs in her headphones, and heads to campus listening to a favorite CD she has had on repeat for weeks.

In class, Annette diligently takes notes in her notebook, although her mind occasionally wanders to thoughts of checking her email later and her evening's study session. She is so grateful that she has a computer, at her apartment, but it was only a few years ago that she relied on the library computers to check email and write her papers. After classes, Annette and her friends head to the college café for lunch, where two TV monitors compete for attention—one blaring a soap opera and the other broadcasting the news. Later that afternoon, she stops by the library to check out several books she'll need for her studies that evening.

Evening transitions smoothly as she returns to her apartment, cooking dinner with her roommates while they discuss their day and laugh over shared memories. As the night progresses, she opens her books and does some assigned reading, then completes several written assignments on her computer saving her work to a flash drive. She then takes a break to send a quick message via her BlackBerry, before settling down to watch her favorite Thursday, 9:00 pm TV show (which is only available one time per week). After the show, she returns to reading one of her library books until she's too sleepy to concentrate, and falls asleep around 11:00 p.m.

Tyler, a 20-year-old college student in 2020

Tyler is awakened by his smart speaker, which blends seamlessly into his morning routine, syncing his schedule and notifying him of the day's tasks. He immediately rolls over, grabs his smartphone, and begins scrolling through social media, checking recent reels, stories, and videos. He then checks his texts and emails, feeling the need to step into his day prepared for all he has to accomplish. A wave of anxiety washes over him before his feet even hit the floor, as he wonders how he is going to manage his daily responsibilities, while also comparing his life with those he follows online. Breakfast is a multitasking affair for him as he watches news streams on his tablet, delivered repeatedly in short, quick waves. Disaster stories, often with detailed video, and political upheavals play out while he preps for his busy day. He catches the bus to campus with earbuds in place, isolating himself in his private bubble, while unconsciously sorting through the information that has flooded his nervous system since the moment he woke.

On campus, lunch is a quick grab from a food truck he randomly passes by between classes, eating in a common area where his peers are half-engaged in conversations and half-checking their phones for the latest trends. Studying means heading to a "smart library," filled with digital textbooks and online resources, ensuring that everything he needs is just a click away. Group projects are often managed via collaborative online tools and virtual meetings, making time flexible yet fragmented. Dinner is ordered through a delivery app, eaten amidst binges of the latest must-watch, streaming series in his shared apartment, where his roommates are similarly glued to their screens. His evening speeds by as he multitasks, flicking between assignments on educational apps, social media, and an online game, before finally unwinding with a meditation app to calm his overstimulated mind. He gives in to sleep around midnight.

These snapshots not only showcase the evolution of technology, but they also highlight the increasing demands and pace of life that have resulted—and the profound impact these changes have had on the daily lives of college students over just a few decades.

A Pervasive Pace of Change

In the world of technology and connectivity, we've moved from using simple analog devices, such as clocks with hour and minute hands, cassette players, radios, and non-digital cameras, to having powerful computers in our pockets (smartphones) that provide all of the above with one quick click. The internet has transformed how we access information, work, and communicate, from the introduction of the World Wide Web, in the early 1990s, to today's high-speed global connectivity.

During previous thirty-year spans, we indeed witnessed transformative advancements in technology, such as the shift from radio to television and the evolution from horse-drawn carriages to automobiles. Yet while these changes were undeniably profound, they did not occur at the exponential rate of transformation that we've experienced in recent decades.

In addition, the shift to digital communications (email, social media, video conferencing) has changed how we work and connect. Remote work, e-commerce, and digital services have become so widespread, we can meet and work with anyone in the world from anywhere. In the past, we progressed relatively slowly from typewriters that used correction tape, to word processors the size of your desk. While these changes were dramatic, they did not affect daily work and communication routines the way the internet has. Social media alone has fundamentally redefined the nature of our relationships and social interactions—reshaping the way we connect, communicate, and share our lives. Instant communications, broader networks, and the blurring of public and private lives have amplified influence, persuasion, and cyberbullying.

Social media alone has fundamentally redefined the nature of our relationships and social interactions.

Over the last three decades, changes such as moving from agrarian to industrial societies (the transition from economies based on agriculture and rural life to those driven by manufacturing, industry, and urbanization) were significant, but also much more gradual—and much less comprehensive in how they affected our personal lives.

In contrast, recent technological changes have vastly changed the way we live, work, and interact. Because of the digital and internet revolution, we can easily communicate globally, work to solve big social problems more collaboratively, and feel more closely connected to friends, family, and co-workers around the world. We have instant access to information through search engines, online libraries, and educational platforms, enabling lifelong learning and awareness. E-commerce and remote working have ushered in flexibility, enhanced work-life balance, and generated new employment opportunities.

We celebrate and applaud all these incredible advancements. It's astounding to think that what once required a room-sized IBM computer can now fit in your pocket. Unlike those massive early machines, today's devices offer instant access to a world of information, a suite of productivity tools, endless entertainment options, and a high-resolution camera that captures stunning photos and videos. Plus, you can effortlessly connect with friends and family across the globe. It's like having an all-in-one technology hub the size of your hand, always at your fingertips.

However, in addition to these helpful advancements, there are also notable disadvantages to being plugged in all the time. Constant digital connectivity has become the norm and the expectation. In the past, connecting took effort—you had to visit a library to use a computer, be home to receive a phone call, and make plans that you stuck to because there was no way to inform others of a change. Now, this perpetual connectivity can lead to heightened stress and anxiety, disrupt sleep patterns, foster a sense of dependency or addiction (when is the last time you navigated a 24-hour period without looking at your smartphone?), dilute the quality of face-to-face relationships, and create constant distractions that hamper productivity and mindfulness. While celebrating the incredible benefits, it's crucial to recognize and manage the drawbacks so you can maintain physical, mental, and emotional health. Yes! We can have both—technological advances *and* mental ease—physical energy *and* emotional balance. However, it does require intentional awareness that can only be achieved through some type of mindfulness practice.

Let's explore the influence of "that" advanced lifestyle and consider "this" intentional and mindful alternative that will bring balance to your digital life *and* physical, mental, emotional, and spiritual life.

THE BUSY BADGE

In today's fast-paced world, being busy has almost become a badge of honor. It's as if there's an unspoken competition to see who can fill their schedules the most, who hustles harder, and who juggles more tasks simultaneously. This glorification of busyness often leads to people equating their worth with their productivity, fostering a culture where downtime is undervalued, and stress is a constant companion. We wear our packed calendars and sleepless nights as proud symbols of our commitment and success, often at the expense of our well-being and deeper, more meaningful connections with others.

Instead of *That,* Do *This*: Instead of wearing your busyness as a badge of honor and subscribing to the myth that relentless pushing to the point of exhaustion, frustration, and burnout defines your value, prioritize intentional and mindful daily check-ins. Each day, take moments to be still, breathe, and engage in self-reflection. Connect with each aspect of your being—physical, mental, emotional, and spiritual—to discern their current state. Listen to the feedback they provide and act accordingly. Perhaps you need more rest or increased activity, more connection with others or solitary reflection, a sense of accomplishment or time immersed in nature. Your body is incredibly insightful and will guide you toward balance and well-being. Your truest answers are within, but to hear them clearly, you must breathe, be still, and go within. Embrace a life of quality and mindful presence rather than one of overwhelm and exhaustion.

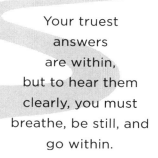

Your truest answers are within, but to hear them clearly, you must breathe, be still, and go within.

MULTITASKING

Many of us believe that juggling multiple tasks at once is necessary, making us more efficient, productive, and effective. However, research consistently shows this isn't the case. Multitasking can actually make us less efficient and more prone to mistakes. Our brains aren't designed to handle several tasks simultaneously; switching back and forth between them creates mental fatigue, increases stress, and decreases effectiveness. This constant shifting between actions—such as eating, scrolling, studying, checking notifications, and conversing—can leave us feeling scattered, fragmented, and exhausted with a diminished ability to focus deeply on any one task. Much like any other behavior, focus is a developed skill, and multitasking stands as the antithesis to honing this vital ability.

Instead of *That*, Do *This*: Instead of scattering your attention across many activities at once, be intentional about what you're doing and build your focus on that one thing. If you're studying, turn off distractions like the TV, close extra browser tabs, and set your phone to "do not disturb." When you're talking with a friend, co-worker, or family member, show them you care by being fully present. Put your phone away, don't respond to texts during the conversation, and enjoy the genuine connection.

CHAOS CONFUSION

Today, many people confuse a lack of chaos with being boring, rather than seeing it as enriching and peaceful. Because of this, they end up filling their lives with unnecessary chaos and busyness, unconsciously mirroring the chaos of others. Over time, their bodies adapt to the constant hustle. When they finally have an opportunity to sit quietly, they experience stress instead of feeling peaceful because their bodies have become accustomed to a state of constant activity. This means that calm moments can make them feel more anxious rather than relaxed. To break this cycle, it's important to start experiencing quiet and stillness as a good thing—something that helps recharge you and brings true peace.

Instead of *That*, Do *This*: Instead of filling your life with constant chaos and mistaking calm as boredom, embrace the peace that comes with stillness. Take moments throughout your day to slow down and just be. If you feel bored, reframe it as an opportunity to recharge rather than a void to fill with more activity. Practice deep breathing, earthing, or simply enjoy a quiet cup of tea. By doing this, you'll help teach your body to release those peace-inducing hormones, making it easier to truly unwind and find balance.

FEELINGS OF ISOLATION

The rising sensation of loneliness in our increasingly digital world is becoming more prevalent. Many of my students have expressed that they feel less at ease in social settings since the pandemic, often remarking, "I feel like I lost my social skills from spending so much time alone." This creates a self-perpetuating cycle of isolation. The discomfort with social interaction fosters anxiety when they do engage with others, leading to continued self-isolation. This prolonged isolation continues to erode their social skills, resulting in even greater anxiety in subsequent social encounters.

Instead of *That*, do *This*: Unplug and connect. Instead of habitually reaching for your phone when you feel uncomfortable in social settings, take a deep breath, unplug, and genuinely connect. When you're in a conversation, practice being truly present. The greatest human desire is to be seen. Your ability to stay engaged—to see others, hear others, and interact meaningfully—is the most valuable gift you can offer and receive. When your phone or watch vibrates with an alert during a conversation, resist the urge to check it. Keep your phone in your pocket and maintain your focus on the person you're with.

I've learned that people will forget what you said, people will forget what you did, but people will never forget how you made them feel.

—MAYA ANGELOU

SLEEP DEPRIVATION

Even though the average amount of sleep college students get today is only about an hour less than in the 1990s (7-8 hours back then vs. 6-7 hours now), sleep problems have become a lot more common. You might find yourself struggling with falling asleep and staying asleep, making it tough to wake up, feel refreshed, and shake the brain fog. Nowadays, digital distractions play a big part in this. Staying up late on your smartphone or laptop messes with your sleep patterns because of the blue light they emit, as well as the overactive brain activity from a day of multitasking. Poor sleep often leads to more reliance on screens for entertainment and companionship, which creates a vicious cycle. This lack of sleep not only hurts your academic performance, but also your overall health, making you more tired, prone to getting sick, and less focused.

Instead of *That*, do *This*: Instead of staying up late scrolling through your phone or watching TV, prioritize a calming bedtime routine. Set a consistent bedtime and wake-up time every day to regulate your body's internal clock. Dim the lights and avoid blue light from screens at least an hour before bedtime to help signal your mind and body that it's time to wind down. Relax during this time by reading a book, taking a warm bath, or practicing mindfulness or deep-breathing exercises. Be realistic with your expectations. If you cannot do this every night, don't fret, but instead commit to two or three nights per week. You get to choose. By making these changes, you can significantly improve your sleep quality and wake up feeling refreshed and ready to face the day.

POOR NUTRITION

Over the past thirty years, there has been a noticeable trend toward low-quality nutrition, inadequate hydration, and over-stimulating substances driven by busy lifestyles and the convenience of fast food and sugary, caffeinated drinks. Poor dietary choices and dehydration can significantly affect your ability to be mindful. When your body lacks essential nutrients and sufficient water, it struggles to function optimally, leading to fatigue, brain fog, and difficulty concentrating. These physical and mental deficits make it challenging to stay present and fully engaged in the moment.

Instead of *That*, do *This*: Instead of eating junk and not drinking enough water, take a moment to appreciate your body for what it is—a fantastic machine doing countless things, most of which you don't even have to think about. You only get one body, from the day you're born to the day you die. Treat it with the love and care it deserves, like it's your best friend—because it is! Make good food and water a priority to support your physical, mental, emotional, and spiritual health. By taking care of your body, you're giving yourself the best chance to thrive and be truly mindful.

LACK OF PHYSICAL ACTIVITY

The American College Health Association's research shows that many college students live a sedentary lifestyle. Studies indicate that around 40-50% of students aren't getting enough physical activity. This lack of movement is linked to several negative health outcomes, including weight gain, reduced cardiovascular fitness, brain fog, and mental health issues, such as increased anxiety and depression. Inactivity leads to more inactivity, creating a continuous negative cycle.

Instead of *That*, do *This*: Instead of getting trapped in the cycle of inactivity, fight the pull of a sedentary, behind-the-screen life. Increase both your pedestrian movement (walking and moving throughout your day) and planned workout sessions. Your body was designed to move, *and* needs a variety of movements—from longer-duration but lower intensity walking sessions, to less long but more vigorous sessions that increase your heart rate (which also elicits endorphins for elevated mental health). And don't forget to complete some strength training a few days per week. Find various cardio and strength-building activities you love doing—that are fun and enjoyable for you. Whether you love to dance or pull yourself up a climbing wall, do it. If you like being part of a team, seek one out. Whether you like to hike or climb, row a boat or ride a skateboard, make the time to do it. When you find the activity you love, you will not only do more of it, but your mind and body will also benefit because of the happy hormones created along the way.

LIVING DISTRACTED

It's becoming increasingly common to see people walking down the streets and sitting on buses with their faces buried in their phones, oblivious to their surroundings. Whether they're texting, scrolling through social media, or navigating with a GPS app, their focus tends to be anywhere but in the world around them. The same is true for driving; despite the obvious dangers, many drivers still glance at their phones for notifications, messages, or directions, putting themselves and others at significant risk. This pervasive habit not only diminishes our awareness and appreciation of what's around us, but also jeopardizes the safety of ourselves and others. By constantly retreating into our digital devices, we miss the chance to engage with the real world, stay present, and connect meaningfully with the people and places we encounter.

Instead of *That,* **do** *This*: Instead of staring at your phone while walking or driving, focus on being present. Look up; ensure observe your surroundings. Engage with the world around you. If you need to use your phone, find a safe spot to stop and check it. By doing this, you'll enhance your safety, ensure the safety of others, and enrich your experiences.

DETACHMENT

Many college students turn to unhealthy coping mechanisms, such as excessive sleeping, drug and/or alcohol use, and procrastination as a form of self-regulation to detach from the stressors of the world. While these behaviors might offer temporary relief, they often result in a cycle of guilt and increased feelings of being lost. Sleeping excessively can lead to missed opportunities and responsibilities, while drug use can have severe physical and mental health consequences. Procrastination, meanwhile, only amplifies anxiety as deadlines loom closer. Instead of providing the desired escape, these actions usually exacerbate feelings of guilt, inadequacy, and confusion, making it even harder to face challenges head-on and find a balanced, fulfilling path forward.

Instead of *That,* **do** *This*: Instead of detaching from the world by sleeping excessively, using drugs, or procrastinating, get honest with yourself and declare that you would like to experience life in a fuller, more expansive way. Start with small actions and do what you can today. You might commit to walking a thousand more steps per day or sign up for a mindfulness and meditation course. Perhaps you decide to decrease your workload so you have more time for self-care, including nature walks or getting together with friends. Another simple practice that doesn't take much time is to complete daily check-ins with your physical, mental, emotional, and spiritual well-being. This practice helps you stay connected with your whole self and will provide insight as to why you are feeling and behaving in certain ways.

When you feel overwhelmed, it can be difficult to reach out to friends, family, or campus counseling services for support—but this action can be your lifeline. Let someone know that you could use a helping hand, a listening heart, and an encouraging word.

Engaging in these positive behaviors will help you build resilience, reduce guilt, and foster a sense of purpose and direction.

BLUE LIGHT

It's common for college students to spend between ten to twelve hours a day engaged with digital devices, including smartphones, laptops, TVs, and gaming consoles. During periods of intensive academic work, this figure can climb even higher. The blue light emitted from these screens—whether from smartphones, tablets, computers, or LED lighting—has been linked to disrupted circadian rhythms, adversely impacting sleep quality. In addition, it can cause eye strain, headaches, and difficulty focusing. Because these symptoms are often subtle and their connection to blue light exposure isn't immediately obvious, they are frequently dismissed or attributed to general fatigue.

Instead of *That*, do *This*: Instead of mindlessly scrolling through your phone and accumulating excessive blue light exposure, strive to be more deliberate with your digital habits. Establish a daily limit for non-essential screen activities, such as browsing social media, so you can reserve your screen time for more essential tasks. Whenever possible, choose alternatives, such as reading a hardcopy book rather than its digital counterpart, or listening to the book online. In addition, use blue light blocking or blue light filter glasses. These glasses are equipped with special lenses that block out or filter blue light emitted by digital screens, thereby reducing eye strain and potentially helping to improve sleep quality.

Avoiding the Pitfalls of Social Media

Social media creates more challenges in our lives than we often realize. The normalization of its influence further confuses and distracts us. These factors can be some of the biggest obstacles to staying mindful. The section below is dedicated to exploring how social media uniquely affects us and how it undermines our ability to stay present and focused.

CONSTANT HYPER-CONNECTIVITY

Social media has revolutionized the way we communicate by making it possible to send messages instantly across the globe. Platforms like WhatsApp, Facebook Messenger, and Snapchat allow us to stay connected with friends and family at any time, breaking down geographical barriers. However, this instant connectivity can also lead to a constant barrage of notifications, making it difficult to disconnect and be present in the moment. A fun concert turns into a missed experience as we post videos on Instagram; a hike is interrupted as we send pictures to a friend via Snapchat; an exhilarating run gets thwarted as we focus on what would be the best-posed picture to post.

Instead of *That*, do *This*: Instead of staying connected to your device at all times, give yourself permission to stay connected to the experience of your moment. For example, when you're at the concert, really be there. Ignore the urge to post pictures and videos on your socials and instead absorb all the feel-goods of the evening. When you are running, enjoy it to the fullest by paying attention to your heart rate, your breath, and the strength of your legs. Consider leaving your phone at home for a stretch. If this is difficult, start with 30-minute increments and begin building to longer periods of time.

BLURRING OF PUBLIC AND PRIVATE LIVES

One of the most significant impacts of social media is the blurring of public and private boundaries. We often share personal moments publicly, offering a curated glimpse into our lives. While this can foster transparency and open communication, it can also lead to privacy concerns and a loss of boundaries.

Instead of *That*, do *This*: Instead of sharing everything about your life, be intentional about what you share. Maintain boundaries that preserve your privacy and personal space, making conscious choices about how much of your life you make public. Release the habit of constantly pondering, "Would this make a good photo for social media?" causing you to steer your experience toward capturing that perfect shot.

SUPERFICIAL INFLUENCE AND MISINFORMATION

Social media platforms have given rise to influencers who can sway public opinion and trends. This power can be used for positive change, such as raising awareness for important causes. However, it can also lead to manipulation and the spread of misinformation.

Instead of *That*, do *This*: Instead of believing everything you see or believing everybody's lives are worry-free and perfect, develop a critical mindset and verify the information you consume. In addition, use your platform responsibly to share accurate information and promote positive change.

CYBERBULLYING

The anonymity and distance provided by social media can sometimes lead to negative behaviors, such as cyberbullying. This can have devastating emotional and psychological impacts on individuals.

Instead of *That*, do *This*: Instead of engaging in screen-time bravery (being courageous because you're hiding behind the screen), ask yourself, "Would I say this to the person if they were in front of me right now?" If the answer is "No," then refrain from posting your comment. In addition, cultivate a positive online environment by standing against cyber-bullying and promoting kindness and empathy. Avoid the impulse to add comments that could hurt others or contribute to a wave of negativity.

DOPAMINE ADDICTION

Dopamine is a neurotransmitter responsible for feeling good. Every time you receive a notification or a "like" on social media, your brain releases dopamine. This creates a rewarding feeling that your brain starts to crave, much like how it responds to other addictive behaviors. Over time, the habit of constantly checking your phone for these little bursts of happiness can become hard to break. The satisfaction we get from a phone notification is fleeting, yet it can create a dependency that pulls you away from more fulfilling, real-world experiences. Understanding this can help you become more mindful of your habits and how you manage your digital and real-world interactions.

Instead of *That*, do *This*: Instead of unconsciously seeking dopamine hits and relying on your phone as your primary source of this feel-good neurotransmitter, intentionally elevate your dopamine levels by engaging in other activities such as exercise, listening to music, eating healthy foods, completing tasks, meditation and mindfulness, spending time in nature, creating something, learning something new, socializing, and/or practicing gratitude.

Life is a series of choices between "instead of that, do this." It's not only about recognizing when the path you're on is, or is not, serving you, but also having the courage to try a different route when needed. While I've shared numerous strategies and examples, there's something uniquely powerful about witnessing how these choices unfold in the real life of a fellow student. Let's jump back into Tyler's journey, a story that's been unfolding throughout this book.

A Note from Tyler

My journey started off pretty rough: a chaotic home life, crazy-long commutes to school, and dealing with a huge lack of confidence. I thought I was handling it by copying the craziness I saw happening around me, but it was like carrying this massive mountain on my back. Trying to keep up just left me burnt out and feeling like a mess inside.

I always knew I had it in me to be more—to do better— but finding a way out of the chaos seemed impossible. It was frustrating and exhausting; feeling so stuck when I desperately wanted to move forward.

The turning point in my life came when I got hit by a car. In that split second, I realized that if I kept going the way I was, I'd end up dropping out of school. That thought completely clashed with the feeling deep inside that I was meant for something more—more happiness, more fulfillment, more confidence.

I didn't know it then, but this journey to Zen would eventually become part of my life story. I am now thankful for the wake-up call that shook me up and made me see things differently, pushing me onto a new path. That new path eventually led me to our Mind Body Awareness course, and honestly, it's been a game-changer.

Even though I had no idea what I was getting into, something just felt right about it. Looking back, I get it now—this kind of clarity comes when I slow down, take a deep breath, and listen to my gut. Like that time I met up with Sam by the pond and saw the little boy and his grandma just enjoying the moment. That inner voice was pointing me in the right direction, toward something that would be good for me.

Even though I had my fair share of doubts during the course, I kept an open mind and tried out stuff like meditation and gratitude. I mean, I could see things starting to get better, so why not, right? And then there was this one time when I had to talk to Professor Donovan, and I noticed I was stuck in a loop of negative thoughts. I used visualization to shift my perspective, and it totally blew my mind how well it worked. That was the moment I became convinced that this mindfulness stuff really works!

The more I practiced, the more I felt my life shift from one big drag to something I actually enjoyed. Those dark days when life felt unbearable became distant memories. And then it hit me: I didn't have to be just another puppet on a string. For the first time, I felt in control of something—heck, my entire life. I was becoming the author of my own story.

One of the coolest things was that people around me—family, friends, co-workers, professors—they all noticed the shift. They'd compliment me on how different and positive I seemed. That recognition lifted me up and fueled me to take things further. So, I decided to teach mindfulness practices to elementary students through my teaching practicum at the university. I wanted to give these kids the head start I wished I'd had at that age.

My journey wasn't just about finding my way, but creating a life filled with purpose, joy, and meaning. By sharing what I learned, I not only transformed my own life, but I inspired others to do the same. Teaching mindfulness to young students became my way of sparking a ripple effect, helping these kids discover their own paths to inner peace and fulfillment. It's been about growth and giving back, showing that personal transformation can echo far beyond our selves. I realized that I had become part of the mindfulness movement!

Bringing It All Together

In this chapter, we've delved into how our digital lifestyles affect our well-being and mindfulness. From social media's omnipresence to poor nutrition and sedentary habits, we've seen how these erode our physical, mental, emotional, and spiritual health. The stories of Matt, Annette, and Tyler highlight how digital demands have reshaped the lives of college students over the past thirty years.

We've discussed the power of intentional actions—such as building real-world connections, staying active, and practicing mindfulness—to counter some of the negative side effects of these modern challenges. Technology isn't the enemy; it brings countless benefits. However, we must be mindful of its downsides.

Remember the Eagle's phrase, *"Often we live our lives in chains, and we never even know we have the key."* I'm here to tell you that you do have the key—you have the power to craft your life by making conscious, mindful choices. Embrace technology's gifts while staying grounded in presence and connection. Design a life full of balance, purpose, and joy one mindful decision at a time.

Now that you've started to embrace the "Instead of *That*, Do *This*" mindset, it's time to take the next step in deepening your mindfulness practices. In the upcoming chapter, we'll explore how short periods of focused time can be used to embed mindfulness into your days for an elevated life. Discover how specifically focusing on mindfulness practices for these brief moments can foster growth, build resilience, and empower you to create lasting positive changes with ease. Get ready to transform these focused intervals into stepping stones for a more mindful and fulfilling life!

TWELVE

THE ZEN ZONE

PROGRESSIVE CHALLENGES TO BUILD MINDFULNESS

*It is not enough to be busy. So are the ants. The question is:
What are we busy about?*

—HENRY DAVID THOREAU

In this final chapter, we put all that we've learned into action with precise, time-focused challenges that are designed to seamlessly integrate into your daily life. Whether you have just a minute or can commit to a three-week journey, each challenge is crafted to reinforce the mindfulness techniques we've discussed and help you cultivate a richer, more centered mindfulness practice. Some tasks will be quick,

in-the-moment exercises, and others will invite a deeper, prolonged commitment, but every single challenge carries the potential to create significant shifts in your well-being. Let's dive
in and start transforming stress into Zen, one focused moment
at a time.

TEN IN-THE-MOMENT ZEN CHALLENGES

Welcome to the quick-start stepping stone for embracing
mindfulness in the whirlwind of college life! You don't need
hours of free time to practice mindfulness—sometimes all
it takes is a minute. In this section, we'll introduce you to simple, in-the-moment challenges you can implement immediately, right where you are. Each of these brief practices is
designed to anchor you in the present moment, reduce stress,
and bring a sense of tranquility to your day-to-day activities.
Let's dive in and discover how these quick mindfulness moments can create immediate, meaningful shifts in your
well-being.

1. **Mindful Breath Break:** Take a moment to pause
and focus on your breathing for one full minute. Complete three, 5-Phase Breaths, breathing deeply through
your nose, and exhaling slowly through your mouth.
Feel the air filling your lungs and then leaving your
body. Notice how this simple act can center you and
bring you into the present moment. If you want to add
to this practice, imagine receiving something you
want—such as greater focus, energy, clarity, peace,
etc.—during your inhale, and then releasing what you
no longer need—such as distracted thinking, fatigue,
stress, or foggy brain—during your exhale.

2. **Gratitude Glance:** While you're walking to your
next class, pick one thing you see around you and mentally express gratitude for it. It could be the beautiful
weather, a blooming flower, or a kind smile from a
passerby. Allow this moment of gratitude to uplift
your mood.

3. Sensory Stop: Wherever you are, take a quick pause to engage fully with your surroundings through your senses. Notice five things you can see, four you can touch, three you can hear, two you can smell, and one you can taste. This practice helps ground you in the present moment. This is a fantastic practice to use if you are feeling anxious, as it brings you back to the moment and reminds your nervous system that you are here, in control.

4. Litter Lift: As you're walking across campus, make it a point to pick up one piece of litter. This small act of kindness not only helps keep your environment clean, but also brings your focus to the present moment and fosters a sense of community responsibility.

5. Minute of Movement: Take sixty seconds to stand up and stretch your body. Focus on each movement, feeling the stretch in your muscles and the way your body responds. This quick practice can refresh your mind and relieve tension.

6. Gratitude Pause: Take a moment to pause, think about, and feel three things you are grateful for in this very moment. They can be as simple as the warmth of the sun, the taste of your coffee, or the supportive text from a friend. Feel the gratitude deeply within you.

7. Compassionate Connection: During your day, make it a point to smile or say "Hello" to a stranger without any expectation of a response. Simply feel the warmth of your friendly gesture and the small connection it creates, no matter the outcome.

8. Mindful Listening: When you are engaged in a conversation, practice mindful listening. Focus fully on the other person, absorbing their words, tone, and expressions. Resist the urge to formulate your response while they are talking; be wholly present in the moment.

9. Nature Noticing: Spend a minute appreciating a natural element around you—a tree, the sky, a flower, or even the sound of birds. Take a moment to count the petals on a flower or mimic the sound of the bird. Allow yourself to fully experience this connection with nature, noticing its beauty and presence.

10. Tension Release: Identify a spot where you're holding tension in your body (like your shoulders, neck, or jaw). Take a deep breath, and as you exhale, consciously release the tension in that area. Feel the relaxation spreading through that part of your body and beyond.

These exercises are crafted to seamlessly integrate mindfulness into your daily routines, offering swift yet potent ways to stay grounded and connected amidst life's chaos. Release the urge to tackle all of them at once. Think of this collection like an all-you-can-eat buffet—some exercises will immediately catch your attention, while others may not appeal to you at all. Start by indulging in the exercises that resonate with you. As you engage with those, you may find yourself gradually drawn to trying out the others, discovering new ways to weave mindfulness into your life.

Another way to approach these short, in-the-moment practices is to randomly choose one. Close your eyes, take a deep breath, and ask yourself, "Which of these practices will serve me the best today?" Then let your finger or pen randomly land on one of them. Trust that you landed on your perfect practice for now, then implement it throughout the day. If you want extra credit, at the end of the day, journal about your experience so you can capture all the nuances and potential magic that happened because of your mindfulness practice.

As we wrap up these brief but powerful practices, remember that it's the small, consistent moments of focus that create the greatest impact over time. By integrating these simple challenges into your daily routine, you're building a foundation of presence and calm that can support you through the busyness and stress of college life. It's not about finding more time—it's about making the most of the moments you already have. Keep these practices handy, revisit them often, and watch how they transform your mindset and enhance your sense of well-being. Here's to living each moment with intention and serenity.

FIVE MULTIPLE-DAY ZEN CHALLENGES

Now that you've dipped your toes into the in-the-moment Zen challenges, you might be eager to embark on a multi-day mindfulness journey. These are designed to extend your practice and help you weave mindfulness into the very fabric of your life over the next few days. Ranging from 3 to 5 days, each challenge is a focused experience aimed at deepening your awareness, enhancing your well-being, and fostering a greater sense of presence. Whether it's through gratitude journaling, mindful eating, digital detoxing, nature walks, or loving-kindness meditation, these exercises will guide you in creating lasting habits that support a more centered and peaceful you. Ready to dive in? When you are, let's embark on these multi-day enriching journeys!

1. **Mindful Eating (3 Days):** For three days, practice mindful eating during one meal each day. Turn off all distractions. Pay close attention to the colors, textures, and flavors of your food. Chew slowly and savor each bite, listening to your body's hunger and fullness cues. Notice how the food makes you feel—i.e., lethargic, energized, bloated, satiated, etc.

It's not about finding more time—it's about making the most of the moments you already have.

2. Loving-Kindness Meditation (4 Days): Dedicate ten minutes each day for the next five days to practicing loving-kindness meditation. Sit comfortably, focus on your breath, and silently repeat phrases such as, "May I be happy; may I be healthy; may I be at peace." Gradually extend these desires toward others—family, friends, acquaintances, and even those you may have conflicts with. Observe any shifts in your heart and attitude toward others by the end of the challenge.

3. Digital Detox Evenings (4 Days): For the next four nights, commit to a digital detox for the last hour before bed. Engage in relaxing activities, such as reading a book, journaling, meditating, or practicing gentle stretches. Turn down the lights, play soft music, and perhaps light a candle (the gentle, flickering candlelight can help to increase melatonin, causing a relaxed, even drowsy feeling). Observe any changes in your sleep quality and overall sense of calm.

4. Gratitude Journal (5 Days): At the end of your day, write down five things for which you are grateful, and then reflect on why you feel grateful for each item. You can use this sentence stem for writing what and why you are grateful: "Something I'm grateful for is

_____

because _____." Notice any shifts in your perspective and mood by the end of these five days.

5. Nature Walks (5 Days): Spend at least twenty minutes a day walking in nature for the next five days. Whether it's a park, a trail, or a tree-lined street, fully immerse yourself in your surroundings. Notice the sights, sounds, and scents of nature, allowing this daily communion to rejuvenate you and bring a sense of peace.

These multi-day challenges are perfect for fitting into a busy schedule while still providing a deep, meaningful opportunity to expand your mindfulness practice. Move into them with the presence of the beginner's mind—open and willing to experience them without expectation or judgment. In addition, make them your own so you get everything you want out of them. If you feel the need to adjust the length of time, do so with intention, creating your own guidelines, but identify those at the beginning of the challenge rather than partway through. Journaling can significantly elevate your experience, so I encourage you to document your journey daily. At the end of your challenge, reflect on your experience by reviewing your daily entries, then write an overview that captures both high-level insights and detailed specifics. This reflective practice will help solidify the growth and learning you've achieved.

FOUR EXTENDED ZEN CHALLENGES

Get ready to dive into our final and most transformative set of challenges—designed to span 7 to 21 days! This is where the extra magic happens. By committing to these extended mindfulness practices, you are truly getting on board with our Mindfulness Movement. Here you will unlock deeper levels of self-awareness, resilience, and inner peace. Imagine waking up each day feeling more grounded, focused, and connected to the present moment. These challenges will help you build lasting habits that nourish your mind, body, and spirit. Though the journey is longer, the rewards are immeasurable—including a more centered, calm, and vibrant you. So gear up and get excited; this is your chance to make profound shifts in your life, one mindful day at a time. When you're ready, let's begin this new amazing adventure!

1. Unplugged Bliss (7 Days): This mindfulness challenge is designed to help you step away from your digital devices and reconnect with the present moment. In a world where we're constantly bombarded with notifications, screens, and digital distractions, taking these intentional breaks can greatly enhance your mental well-being, focus, and presence. **The Challenge:** For the next week, commit to practicing a brief digital detox once a day—for a period of 30 to 60 minutes during a specific activity (or longer). Here are steps to guide you through this challenge:

Choose Your Time Slot. Decide on a specific 30 to 60-minute window each day when you will completely disconnect from all digital devices. This could be during a meal, while walking, or while engaging in a hobby like reading, cooking, drawing, or working out.

Set Your Intention. Before you begin, take a moment to set a clear intention for your digital detox. Return to Chapter 6 to review how to set clear intentions. Remember to identify how you want to feel before describing the actions you will take.

Notify and Disconnect. Let anyone important know that you'll be unreachable for the next 30 to 60 minutes and switch off your devices. Put your phone, laptop, and any other digital gadgets in a different room, or at least on "Do Not Disturb" mode.

Engage Fully with Your Chosen Activity. Dive deeply into your chosen activity with your full attention. Here are a few suggestions for activities:

- **Mealtime** - Savor your food mindfully, paying close attention to the flavors, textures, and colors. Enjoy the dining experience without the distraction of a screen.
- **Nature Walk** - Go for a walk in nature without your phone. Notice the sights, sounds, and scents around you. Allow the natural environment to refresh and center you.

- **Hobby Time** - Engage in a hobby you love—painting, playing a musical instrument, gardening, or reading a book. Focus fully on the joy and creativity of your activity without digital interference.
- **Conversational Focus** - Spend time with a friend or family member, giving them your undivided attention. Listen carefully to what they're saying and engage in meaningful conversation.
- **Driving** - While driving, commit to not looking at or engaging with your phone. You might enjoy taking it to the next level by turning off your radio and simply enjoying the hum of the engine and the vibration of the tires.
- **Mindful Presence.** Throughout your digital detox period, keep bringing your awareness back to the present moment. Notice how it feels to be fully engaged in your activity without the lure of digital distractions.
- **Reflect and Journal.** After your 30 to 60-minute detox, take a few minutes to reflect on your experience. You might want to journal about:

  - How it felt to disconnect from digital devices
  - Any changes in your mood or mental clarity
  - What you noticed or appreciated about your chosen activity
  - How you can incorporate more mindful moments of digital detox in your daily *routine*

Gradual Integration. Over the week, you might find that this practice of mindful disconnection becomes easier and more enjoyable. Consider finding more opportunities throughout your day to step away from screens and reconnect with the present moment.

Daily Reflection. At the end of each day, jot down a few thoughts in your journal about how your digital detox impacted your day. Notice any patterns or changes in your overall well-being, focus, and mood.

By embracing this unplugged bliss, you're taking an essential step toward creating healthier boundaries with technology and reclaiming your presence and peace. Enjoy these moments of simplicity and mindfulness and let them enhance your everyday life.

Upon completion of the ten days, journal about your experience. What did you notice during this time? Was it stressful, peaceful, or something in between? When was it the hardest and when was it the easiest? Is this something you want to continue incorporating into your life? Which elements are most important for you to integrate?

2. Serenity Sunrise (10 Mornings)

Over the next ten days, you will cultivate a consistent morning mindfulness practice designed to set a calm, focused, and positive tone for the rest of your day. By repeating the same practice each morning, you'll deepen your mindfulness skills and create a powerful habit that supports your well-being.

Mindful Breathing and Meditation (10 minutes): Start each day with ten minutes of mindful breathing and meditation. Abstain from looking at your phone or engaging in other outside-oriented activities until you complete your practice. Find a quiet, comfortable space where you won't be disturbed. In an effort to increase your awareness and energy for the day, I recommend sitting for this rather than lying down. Close your eyes and focus entirely on your breath. Begin with three, 5-Phase Breaths. Let go of any tension or distractions and allow your mind to settle. Maintain your focus on your breath, gently bringing your attention back whenever it wanders.

Gratitude Reflection (5 minutes): Immediately after your meditation, spend five minutes reflecting on three things you are grateful for. Write them down in a journal or simply think about them deeply. Consider why each one is meaningful to you and how it adds value to your life. This practice will help shift your mindset towards positivity and appreciation.

Gentle Morning Stretch (10 minutes): Engage in a gentle, mindful stretch or yoga routine. Focus on the sensations in your body, your breathing, and your movements. This practice will invigorate your body, increase your flexibility, and promote a sense of physical and mental relaxation.

Reflect and Journal: Take a few minutes to reflect on your morning practice. Write down any observations, feelings, or insights you experienced through this practice.

End of Day Reflection: At the end of your day, during your sleep-prep time (all electronics turned off, lights turned down low, soft music in the background), journal about your day. Notice how your morning mindfulness routine is impacting your overall mood, focus, and well-being.

Final Reflection (Day 10): On the last day of the challenge, spend extra time reflecting on your entire ten-day journey. Review your journal entries and summarize the changes you've noticed in yourself. Write about the benefits you've experienced and how you plan to continue incorporating mindfulness into your daily routine.

By the end of these ten days, you'll have established a powerful morning mindfulness practice that will leave you feeling more centered, positive, and equipped to handle the challenges of the day. Enjoy this journey of repetitive practice and self-discovery and watch how it transforms your mornings and beyond!

3. The Focused Fortnight (14 Days)

Welcome to the Focused Fortnight! For the next fourteen days, you will embark on a journey to mindful mastery through the practice of mindful movement. Each day, you will dedicate thirty minutes to engaging in activities such as yoga, tai chi, or mindful walking—immersing yourself fully in the sensations and rhythms of your body and breath. This consistent practice will help you build greater awareness, improve your physical well-being, and deepen your connection to the present moment. Let's dive in and explore each element of this transformative challenge.

Mindful Movement Practice (30 minutes): Choose one of the activities below and immerse yourself in it for the next thirty minutes.

Yoga: Select a series of yoga poses or follow a guided yoga routine. Focus on the alignment of your body, your breath, and the flow between poses. Allow yourself to fully experience the stretch, strength, and relaxation each pose brings.

Tai Chi: Engage in a tai chi routine, flowing through the slow, deliberate movements with mindful awareness. Pay attention to the sensations in your muscles, the grounding of your feet, and the coordination of your breath with each movement.

Mindful Walk: Take a walk in a park, on a trail, or around your neighborhood. Concentrate on the feeling of your feet touching the ground, the movement of your legs, and the natural rhythm of your breath. Notice the sights, sounds, and smells around you, staying fully present in the experience.

Key Focus Areas During Movement

- **Body Sensations:** Tune into the physical sensations in your muscles, joints, and skin. Notice any areas of tension or relaxation, warmth or coolness, and how your body responds to movement.
- **Breathing:** Synchronize your breath with your movements. Breathe deeply and evenly, maintaining a

steady rhythm. Notice how your breath supports your movement and enhances your focus.

- **Rhythm:** Pay attention to the natural rhythm of your movements. Whether you're flowing between yoga poses, moving through tai chi, or walking mindfully, feel the ebb and flow, balance, and harmony in each action.

Journaling and Reflection (5 minutes): After your thirty-minute mindful movement session, spend five minutes journaling about your experience. Reflect on the following questions:

- *How did the mindful movement impact your physical state? Did you notice any changes in tension, flexibility, or energy levels?*

- *How did the practice affect your mental state? Did you feel more focused, relaxed, or peaceful?*

- *Were there any particular moments or sensations that stood out to you during your practice?*

- *How do you feel now, compared to before the session?*

Evening Reflection: Each evening, take a few minutes to review your journal entries from the day. Reflect on any patterns you notice, such as how your body and mind responded to different activities or how your overall well-being is evolving throughout the challenge.

Final Reflection (Day 14): On the last day, take extra time to reflect on your entire 14-day journey. Review your journal entries and summarize the changes and benefits you've experienced. Write about your key takeaways, any challenges you faced, and how you plan to continue incorporating mindful movement into your daily routine.

By completing the Focused Fortnight, you'll have developed a strong foundation in mindful movement, enhancing your physical and mental well-being. This practice not only fosters greater self-awareness, but also promotes a sense of calm and balance that can carry you through life's challenges. Enjoy this transformative journey and embrace the mindful mastery you cultivate!

4. Zen Odyssey (21 Days)

Welcome to the Zen Odyssey Challenge! Over the next twenty-one days, you will embark on an enriching journey designed to deepen your mindfulness practice and bring balance, awareness, and serenity into your daily life. Each day introduces a different practice that can be completed in 10 to 15 minutes, or in brief pauses throughout the day. Enjoy the journey as you explore a variety of mindfulness techniques.

WEEK ONE:
Building Foundations

Day 1 - Mindful Breathing: Begin your day with ten minutes of mindful breathing. Sit comfortably, close your eyes, and focus on the rhythm of your breath. Inhale deeply through your nose, hold for a moment, and then exhale slowly through your mouth. Allow your mind to quiet and embrace the stillness.

Day 2 - Gratitude Reflection: Spend ten minutes writing down three things you are grateful for. Reflect on why you are thankful for these things and how they enhance your life. Use the sentence stem: I am grateful for _____ because _____. Begin again with each gratitude. Allow this gratitude practice to fill your heart with warmth and positivity.

Day 3 - Gentle Morning Stretch: Engage in a gentle fifteen-minute stretch or yoga routine. Focus on your body's sensations as you move and breathe deeply into each stretch. This mindful movement will help invigorate your body and mind.

Day 4 - Body Scan Meditation: Take fifteen minutes to practice a body scan meditation. Starting from your toes and working your way up to your head, focus on each part of your body, noticing any sensations or tension.

Day 5 - Mindful Listening: Choose a piece of calming music or a guided meditation and spend ten minutes fully immersing yourself in the experience. Focus on the sounds and notice how they resonate within you. Allow this practice to set a peaceful tone for your day.

Day 6 - Mindful Eating: For one meal today, practice eating mindfully. Pay close attention to the colors, textures, and flavors of your food. Chew slowly and savor each bite.

Day 7 - Positive Affirmations: Spend ten minutes writing and repeating positive affirmations. Choose statements that resonate with you, such as, "I am calm and centered" or "I am capable of handling whatever comes my way." Repeat these affirmations out loud.

WEEK TWO:
Deepening Awareness

Day 8 - Nature Connection: Step outside for an intentional ten minutes to connect with nature. Feel the cool morning air on your skin, listen to the sounds of birds chirping, and observe the world waking up around you. This connection with nature can ground you and bring a sense of peace. If you cannot go outside, you can walk through your space, connecting with the plants or other live elements in your home, like your dog, cat, bird, etc. If these are unavailable, you can watch a nature video or listen to a nature audio featuring bird sounds, ocean waves, or a rainstorm.

Day 9 - Mindful Journaling: Spend fifteen minutes writing freely in a journal. Reflect on your thoughts, emotions, and any dreams you might have had. Allow the writing to reflect your stream of consciousness, helping you clear your mind and set your intentions for the day.

Day 10 - Mindful Sipping: Prepare a cup of tea or coffee and savor it mindfully. Spend ten minutes focusing on the aroma, taste, and warmth of your drink. Let this experience be a moment of calm and enjoyment, bringing you fully into the present moment.

Day 11 - Mindful Walking: Spend twenty minutes walking mindfully. Focus on the sensations in your feet and body as you walk. Notice the sights, sounds, and smells around you.

Day 12 - Visualization: Spend ten minutes visualizing your ideal day. Close your eyes and imagine yourself moving through your day with ease, focus, and joy. Visualize overcoming any challenges with grace and ending the day feeling accomplished and content.

Day 13 - Positive Affirmations: Spend ten minutes writing and repeating positive affirmations. Choose statements that resonate with you and repeat them with conviction.

Day 14 - Digital Detox Evening: For the last hour before bed, unplug from all digital devices. Spend this time doing a calming activity, such as taking a warm bath, stretching, or meditating.

Week Three:
Cultivating Presence

Day 15 - Reflective Journaling: Spend fifteen minutes reflecting on your week. Write about your experiences, any challenges you faced, and the insights you gained.

Day 16 - Mindful Listening: Choose a piece of calming music or a guided meditation and spend ten minutes fully immersing yourself in the sounds. Notice how your body and mind respond.

Day 17 - Loving-Kindness Meditation: Dedicate ten minutes to a loving-kindness meditation. Begin with yourself, then extend your wishes of happiness, health, and peace to others.

Day 18 - Mindful Conversations: Engage in a conversation with someone while practicing mindful listening. Focus entirely on what they are saying without interrupting or formulating your response.

Day 19 - Animal Connection: Spend fifteen minutes mindfully connecting with an animal. Sit with them and enjoy their calm presence. Sync your breath with theirs and notice how this feels. If you don't have access to a pet consider volunteering at your local shelter.

Day 20 - Compassionate Self-Talk: Spend ten minutes practicing compassionate self-talk. Replace any negative self-talk with kind, supportive, and encouraging words.

Day 21 - Kind Acts: Perform three acts of kindness today, whether it's complimenting someone, helping a stranger, or doing a small favor. Reflect on how these acts make you feel.

Completion - Self-Reflection Journaling: Reflect on your 21-day journey. Spend twenty minutes journaling about your overall experience, the growth you've observed, and how you intend to integrate these mindfulness practices into your daily life moving forward. Which practices were easy for you? Which were difficult? What made them so? What did you learn about yourself, and what did you learn about the practice of mindfulness?

Congratulations! You've completed the Zen Odyssey: A 21-Day Mindfulness Journey. Each practice, reflection, and moment of presence over the past three weeks has collectively laid the foundation for a more mindful and serene life. Take pride in the commitment you've shown and the growth you've achieved. Here's to the journey of continuous improvement, one mindful challenge at a time!

Bringing It All Together

Embracing both short and extended challenges can profoundly enhance your mindfulness practice, enriching your life in countless ways. Whether it's the quick, in-the-moment mindfulness of our "Digital Detox" or the more immersive experience of the "21-Day Zen Odyssey," each challenge offers unique opportunities to cultivate awareness, reduce stress, and foster inner peace. Short challenges, like picking up a piece of litter or practicing mindful breathing, can seamlessly fit into your daily routine, providing immediate grounding and centeredness. On the other hand, extended challenges, such as engaging in mindful movement for The Focused Fortnight, or committing to a structured morning routine with Serenity Sunrise, allow you to build deeper, more lasting habits that transform your overall well-being. By undertaking these challenges, you're dedicating yourself to meaningful growth and self-discovery, crafting a more mindful, balanced, and serene life.

Remember, mindfulness is an ongoing journey—a practice to carry with you, adapt, and deepen as you progress. Reflect on the insights you've gained and the positive shifts you've experienced in your daily life—whether through all or a few of the invitations offered here. Continue to nurture your mindfulness practice, knowing that the benefits will resonate long after you've completed it. Here's to a future filled with greater awareness, enduring balance, and a state of Zen. Keep exploring and savoring every mindful moment.

FROM STRESSED TO ZEN
MINDFULNESS POST-ASSESSMENT

Now that you have completed your transformative mindfulness journey, let's take a moment for some self-reflection. This mindfulness post-assessment is designed to help you gauge how far you've come. Think of it as a personal check-in to acknowledge the progress you've made and the growth you've experienced. By reflecting on your answers now, you'll gain valuable insight into the positive changes in your habits and mindset. This reflection will also help reinforce the new skills you've developed and highlight areas to continue working on. I suggest you complete the post-assessment without looking back at your post-assessment.

Ready to begin?

> **Instructions:** For each statement below, please circle the number that best describes how often you experience each situation.

1 = Rarely or Never | **2** = Occasionally | **3** = Sometimes
4 = Often | **5** = Almost Always

1. AWARENESS OF BREATH: I consciously notice and focus on my breath throughout the day.

1   2   3   4   5

2. ENGAGING WITH NATURE: I spend time in nature to relax and rejuvenate.

1   2   3   4   5

3. NONJUDGMENTAL OBSERVATION: I observe my thoughts and feelings without judging them.

1   2   3   4   5

4. EATING FOR HEALTH AND ENERGY: I make mindful food choices that support my overall health and energy levels.

1   2   3   4   5

5. PRESENT MOMENT AWARENESS: I fully experience and engage with the present moment, rather than getting lost in thoughts about the past or future.

1   2   3   4   5

6. STRESS RESPONSE: When I feel stressed, I use mindfulness techniques to help calm myself down.

1   2   3   4   5

7. NURTURING SLEEP: I prioritize getting enough restful sleep and maintaining a consistent sleep routine.

1   2   3   4   5

8. ACCEPTANCE: I accept things as they are without immediately trying to change them.

1   2   3   4   5

9. EMOTIONAL AWARENESS: I am aware of my emotions as they arise and can name them accurately.

1   2   3   4   5

10. ASKING FOR HELP: I reach out for support when I need help or am feeling overwhelmed.

1   2   3   4   5

11. **BODY AWARENESS:** I pay attention to physical sensations in my body without judging them.

1   2   3   4   5

12. **MINDFUL COMMUNICATION:** I listen fully when others are speaking, without planning my response while they talk.

1   2   3   4   5

13. **REACTIVITY:** I notice when I'm reacting automatically and try to respond more mindfully.

1   2   3   4   5

14. **COMPASSION:** I treat myself with kindness and understanding when I'm going through a difficult time.

1   2   3   4   5

Scoring Instructions: To reveal your overall mindfulness profile, simply add up the numbers you've circled for each statement. This total will give you a sense of where you currently stand on the path toward greater mindfulness. Think of it as a snapshot that captures your current state, providing a foundation for growth as you move forward.

- **14-28:** You might still find it challenging to incorporate mindfulness practices into your daily life.

- **29-42:** You have some mindfulness awareness, but there's room for growth.

- **43-56:** You're fairly aware and practicing mindfulness regularly. Continued practice will help you refine your techniques and broaden your understanding.

- **57-70:** You have a strong mindfulness practice!

Thank you for taking the time to complete this post-assessment. Now that you have completed it, compare your results with your pre-assessment. What did you notice? What caught your attention? Which areas improved? Which areas would benefit from more attention?

As a reminder, there is no right or wrong—it's all valuable insight, and *you* get to choose how you will address that insight. Remember, mindfulness is a continuous journey, and celebrating your progress is just as important as setting new goals. Embrace this moment as a testament to your growth and newfound awareness. Each step you've taken has contributed to your unique path of mindfulness and well-being.

CONGRATULATIONS!

Y ou have completed your mindfulness journey from
stressed to Zen! Thank you for embarking upon this
journey with us. *You* are already making a difference in your
life and in the lives of others, and we all thank you for that.
A centered *you* impacts the world—because you *are* the
MINDFULNESS MOVEMENT!

ACKNOWLEDGMENTS

First and foremost, I want to express my deepest gratitude to the students and clients I have had the privilege to work with over the decades. Your curiosity, open-mindedness, and enthusiasm have been the driving force behind this work.

I am immensely grateful to my editor and writing coach, Melissa Killian, whom I synchronistically met on a mindfulness hike in Boulder, CO. Melissa's wisdom, guidance, and support have provided a solid foundation for this journey. My heartfelt thanks also go out to our designer, Rob Williams, and to all my friends, who have been my biggest cheerleaders, especially my partner Charlie. His unwavering support, patience, and physical, mental, and emotional nourishment fueled me through countless deep-dive writing marathons.

Writing *From Stressed to Zen* has been both a personal journey and a professional endeavor. The insights and practices shared within these pages have transformed my own life, and I am thrilled to share them with you.

To everyone who believed in me even when doubts clouded my vision, thank you. Your faith was my compass, guiding me toward completion.

Finally, to each and every reader, thank you for taking this step toward a more mindful and serene life. The journey *From Stressed to Zen* is one we're on together. From the bottom of my heart, thank you for your interest in connecting mindfully with yourself and others, as we all continue to nurture our Mindfulness Movement.

NOTES

1. Merriam-Webster. (n.d.). Wholistic. In *Merriam-Webster.com dictionary*. Retrieved (9/1/24), from https://www.merriam-webster.com/dictionary/wholistic

2. Merriam-Webster. (n.d.). Paradigm. In *Merriam-Webster.com dictionary*. Retrieved (9/1/24), from https://www.merriam-webster.com/dictionary/paradigm

3. Kaplan, R., & Kaplan, S. (1989). *The Experience of Nature: A Psychological Perspective*. Cambridge University Press.

4. Li, Q., Otsuka, T., Kobayashi, M., Wakayama, Y., Inagaki, H., Katsumata, M., Shimizu, T., Hirata, Y., Li, Y.J., Hirata, K., Suzuki, H., Kuwahara, T., Kagawa, T., & Miyazaki, Y. (2011). Acute effects of walking in forest environments on cardiovascular and metabolic parameters. *European Journal of Applied Physiology*, 111, 2845-2853. https://doi.org/10.1007/s00421-011-1918-z

5. Bratman, G. N., Hamilton, J. P., Hahn, K. S., Daily, G. C., & Gross, J. J. (2015). Nature experience reduces rumination and subgenual prefrontal cortex activation. *Proceedings of the National Academy of Sciences, 112*(28), 8567–8572. https://doi.org/10.1073/pnas.1510459112

Made in the USA
Monee, IL
07 January 2025

76345037R00125